Sacred Mountains of China

Sacred Mountains of China

Four Sacred Mountains, One Remarkable Human-Powered Adventure

RYAN PYLE

London, United Kingdom

Sacred Mountains of China
© Copyright 2015 by Ryan Pyle Productions Limited
All rights reserved.
ISBN-13: 978-0992864415
ISBN-10: 0992864415

Ryan Pyle Productions books may be purchased for educational, business, or sales promotional use. For information, please write: Special Markets, Ryan Pyle Productions Limited: First Floor Radius House, 51 Clarendon Road, Watford, Hertfordshire, United Kingdom.

FIRST EDITION
Interior designed by Chris Crochetière, BW&A Books, Inc.
Cover designed by Jonathan Hogan.
Cover Photograph by Ryan Pyle (Top); Chad Ingraham (Bottom); Ryan Pyle (Portrait).

Library of Congress Cataloging-in-Publication Data
Pyle, Ryan
Sacred Mountains of China: Four Sacred Mountains,
One Remarkable Human-Powered Adventure / Ryan Pyle.
p. cm.
ISBN 978-0992864415
1. China—Description and Travel.
2. Adventure Travel.
3. Tibet—Description and Travel.
4. Buddhism—Description and Travel.
China. I. Title

When you are thousands of meters above sea level,
on the side of a remote mountain where there are no roads,
no other people and no phone or Internet access,
there is only one way down.

Contents

Thousands of tired, nerve-shaken, over-civilized people are beginning to find out that going to the mountains is going home; that wildness is a necessity; and that mountain parks and reservations are useful not only as fountains of timber and irrigating rivers, but as fountains of life.

[JOHN MUIR, naturalist, adventurer and activist, 1838–1914]

The Concept Develops

I knew before I set out in July 2013 that each of the treks I was planning to make around four of China's most sacred mountains would present its own unique set of challenges. By the time I completed the last journey just four months later, I had been pushed to the very limits of my physical and mental endurance, and I returned to Shanghai a different man.

In every walk with nature one receives far more than he seeks.
[JOHN MUIR]

During my second year as a student of international politics at the University of Toronto, I completed a course entitled 'An Introduction to Modern China.' I had selected it at random to make up the required number of credits, but it sparked an interest and I took more China-related courses the following year. By the time I graduated in 2001 at the age of 22, I had already made plans to visit the country that was to become my home.

Surprisingly perhaps, I wasn't at all daunted by my inability to speak or understand a word of Chinese; quite the reverse in fact: I relished the opportunity of having to be independent and self-sufficient. I thought that living on my wits while traveling alone for three months might help me to reach some conclusions about what I wanted to do for the rest of my life—or, at least, for the next few years of it.

I tied up all the loose ends in Toronto, booked my flight to China, and was as ready as I would ever be to set out on my first big adventure when the 9/11 terrorist attacks occurred in New York and Washington. Suddenly, North Americans weren't flying anywhere unless they absolutely had to. I'm sure my parents would have been relieved if I had told them I'd cancelled my trip. I know they were worried when I said I was going ahead as planned. I expect they would have been even more anxious if they had known that I was intending to visit Xinjiang, a province in western China that borders Afghanistan and had just become the target of bomb attacks by the US and its allies following 9/11.

Fortunately, my parents' fears for my safety proved unfounded and even now, 13 years later, going to China remains one of the best decisions I've ever made.

From my own perspective, the timing of the trip couldn't have been better. I had financial help from my parents during my four years at university, and I worked through every holiday, so I was lucky enough to have graduated without any debts. And as I didn't have a mortgage, wasn't married, and didn't have kids, I had no responsibilities of any kind. As a result, I had none of the usual financial pressures that push young people into work before they've had a chance to reflect on who they really are or, perhaps even more importantly, who they *want* to be. I think I suspected even then that once you step onto the treadmill of employment, it gathers speed until you can't even imagine trying to jump off.

It wasn't that I was unhappy with my life in Canada. It was just that I had reached the age of 22 without ever having traveled outside North America and Western Europe and didn't want to settle down and get a job before I had seen at least some small part of what else was out there.

My interest in China was further fueled by the fact that it was somewhere completely 'foreign', in the sense of being unfamiliar and unknown. What I couldn't have anticipated was that being in China would be like waking up after spending the last few years sleepwalking. In China, I felt as though I was a 'better version' of myself. And that made me realize I didn't want an 'easy' life: I wanted my life to be full of new experiences and challenges so that I wouldn't ever forget that I could always try harder and do better.

Throughout the months when I was traveling around China, I kept a diary and wrote long letters to my family and friends back at home, describing all the things I was seeing and experiencing.

And that's what triggered my second major epiphany, which is that I enjoy documenting and sharing my experiences with other people and needed to find some way of incorporating that enjoyment into whatever work I was going to do.

Another revelation I had was that, notwithstanding my respectful wariness of wild animals—which some, hyper-critical, people might say borders on outright fear—I have a very strong sense of connection with the natural world. For someone who likes to manage my own endeavors, I was surprised to find how much I enjoyed exploring remote mountain regions where, as the going gets tough, nature takes control.

In 2002, the year after my first visit to China, I left Canada again, not on an adventure of finite duration this time, but to make my home in Shanghai. As soon as I arrived I knew I was in the place I wanted to be. I worked initially as an English teacher, while trying to figure out what I really wanted to do. When it finally dawned on me, I quit my job as a language teacher and started working as a photographer. Before long, I was doing assignments for some major newspapers and magazines, including the *New York Times, TIME, Newsweek,* and *Fortune* in the US, and the *Sunday Times* in the UK.

Working as a photographer involved traveling extensively, at a time when China was going through a period of rapid, unprecedented change and evolution. I derived a great deal of satisfaction from being able to document and share with the outside world some aspects of what was happening in the country. Every year, I tried to come up with at least one idea for an assignment that would take me back to the remote mountain regions of western China that had fascinated me during my first visit in 2001. The images I captured during all those visits became the subject of my own long-term project, which culminated recently in the publication of my first photography book, *Chinese Turkestan.*

By the time my brother Colin and I set out to circumnavigate China on BMW motorcycles in 2010, I thought I knew the country pretty well. One of the many things I learned on that journey, however, is that even if you were to travel around China for a whole lifetime, you wouldn't see it all.

The trip turned into an epic adventure. Between the day when

Colin and I decided it would be cool to spend some time traveling together and the day when we actually set out, our plans evolved and expanded to include my friend and talented professional cameraman Chad Ingraham. Chad drove a support vehicle and filmed our journey for what became a six-part TV documentary series that was broadcast around the world on Travel Channel, Netflix, and iTunes.

Almost exactly two years after we had set out on our journey around China, Colin and I rode out of Delhi on locally manufactured Royal Enfield motorcycles to begin a circumnavigation of India. Again, Chad came with us, this time accompanied by an assistant cameraman and driver. The six-part TV documentary series that resulted from that journey also aired around the world on Travel Channel, Netflix, and iTunes and was the subject of our second book, entitled *The India Ride*.

The tremendous amount of positive feedback and support we received both during and after those two journeys was hugely encouraging. Knowing that what we'd done had inspired people to have adventures of their own—even if it was only heading off somewhere different for a weekend—was something that, inspired *me*. For someone who loves to document and share his experiences, it was clear that I had found what I wanted to do.

Not long before we set out on our circumnavigation of China, Colin had come to a crossroads in his work in finance in Canada. When we embarked on 'The India Ride', he had just completed an MBA in London, England. For him, the journeys we had done together were a brief divergence from his 'real' life in London, where he lives with his wife and has business interests of his own. So, after India, I had a choice to make: I could do another motorcycle journey on my own, or I could do something similar, but different.

One of the advantages of traveling by motorcycle rather than car is that you're more connected with your environment. But even on a motorcycle you're moving faster than the world around you, so most of your attention is focused on the road. What you're also thinking about are the many uncertainties, such as where you need to end up that day, when (sometimes *if*) you're going to get there, whether you have enough gas to make it to the next gas station—

Tibet

North-east of the Himalayas and with an average elevation of 4900 m (16,000 feet) ASL, the Tibetan Plateau is the highest area of land on Earth and the source of several important rivers, including the Yangtze, Yellow River, Mekong, Ganges, Indus, Brahmaputra and Nujiang.

Established as a nominally unified, single empire in the 7th century, the country was subsequently divided into numerous territories and warring principalities. Parts of Tibet were ruled at different times by Mongol and Chinese overlords, and its borders changed repeatedly until the 18th century.

In 1951, Tibet was incorporated into China. In 1965, the Tibet Autonomous Region was created from its western and central areas, and the rest of the region was incorporated as ethnic autonomous prefectures into the Chinese provinces of Sichuan, Yunnan and Qinghai.

As well as indigenous Tibetans, the region is home to numerous ethnic groups and has substantial populations of Han and Hui Chinese. In addition to the primary religion of Buddhism, there are also Bon, Muslim, and Christian minorities.

The economy of Tibet Autonomous Region is largely dependent on subsistence agriculture and, more recently, tourism.

which might be hundreds of kilometers away—or enough money to cover the costs of any substantial delays to your schedule.

I guess those were some of the reasons why I wanted my next adventure to be both mentally and physically challenging and to enable me to have a truly intimate connection with my environment. The more I thought about it, the closer I came to the realization that there was one obvious option: trekking in the mountains. The film footage of Colin and I traveling together was at least partly dependent on the interaction between us. This time, the only thing that would really matter would be the environment itself.

I've loved walking in the mountains ever since I came to live in China. Somehow, it always feels like going home. So, why not incorporate that into my next 'great adventure', raise the bar, increase the challenge, and circumnavigate some of the country's highest and most sacred mountains?

After giving it some thought, I chose four mountains in western

China: Minya Konka, which is the highest mountain in Sichuan Province; Amne Machin in Qinghai Province; Mount Kailash in Tibet Autonomous Region; and Kawa Karpo, the highest mountain in Yunnan Province and one of the most sacred to Tibetan Buddhists. All four mountains are in the plateau region of Tibet.

The plan was to circumambulate all four mountains over a period of four months, between July and October. Each trek would be a secular facsimile of a *kora*, a meditative pilgrimage that is performed every year around sacred mountains, lakes, and manmade structures such as monasteries and temples by tens of thousands of Buddhist, Bon, Hindu, and Jain pilgrims.

Although I didn't expect my treks around the sacred mountains to be rewarded by a multitude of blessings and I wasn't hoping, specifically, to purify my karma, I have a great deal of respect for the pilgrims who do hold those beliefs. And I can certainly understand why someone searching for enlightenment—religious or otherwise—might look for it in remote mountainous regions where humankind has not (yet) left its indelible mark.

There are other holy mountains in Tibet and western China, so why choose those four? The answer is because they are all relatively accessible, have trek-able trails, and could be circumambulated without putting ourselves in extreme danger.

Another appealing aspect of trekking in the mountains was the physical and mental challenge that would be involved in pushing myself to new limits of endurance. It's an opportunity most people living in the West today never have—or rarely take advantage of. What I also relished was the prospect of separating myself for a few days from the rapid pace of city life in Shanghai and reconnecting with the natural world.

I knew I wouldn't find God in the sacred mountains. My only hope and expectation was that I would have an adventure—as I'd had on the motorcycle journeys. It would be overstating it to say I 'found myself', but it's certainly true to say that I made a few personal discoveries that had a subtle yet profound effect on me.

It was because of my love of the mountains that I developed an interest in the Scottish-American naturalist John Muir. Born in 1838, Muir played a pivotal role in setting up national parks in

---

Bon

The origins of the Bon religion are uncertain. Some people believe that Buddhism developed from it and that it was first practiced in Tibet and amongst Tibetans in Nepal many thousands of years ago. Others consider it to be a much later offshoot of Tibetan Buddhism.

Based on primarily shamanistic and animistic traditions and on the worship of nature, Bon has at its center five 'pure lights'—earth, fire, water, air, and space—each of which has its own physical properties and is related to a particular sense and emotion.

In 1978, after many years of competition between the Bon and Buddhist religions, Bon was finally acknowledged by the Dalai Lama to be separate and distinct.

Of the 300 Bon monasteries in Tibet prior to its incorporation into China in 1951, 264 still remain and it is estimated that 10% of Tibetans are Bonpo—the name given to followers of the Bon religion.

---

the USA. As a result, areas such as Yosemite Valley and the Sierra Nevada mountains were secured against future development, and conservation areas were subsequently established in many other countries. 'Salvation can be found through immersion in the natural world,' Muir said. Having completed my treks around four of China's sacred mountains, I finally understood what he meant.

In my 'normal' life, I love the purposeful hustle of the city. I've always been the type of person who *needs* to keep moving: I only ever sit down to work at my computer or eat a meal. I'm very happy to embrace new technology and I acknowledge, with awe and appreciation, the fact that it has completely transformed our lives, particularly during the last 20 years or so. I also have respect for, but do not wish to emulate, the lives of the Amish, and just to clarify I am not a New Age tree-hugger. What I do believe, however, is that we should make huge efforts to ensure that the inevitable and, in many ways for many people, beneficial march of progress doesn't proceed at the cost of destroying everything in its path.

Although each of the journeys I made around the sacred mountains had its own unique set of challenges, they all followed a similar basic pattern. On day one, I would feel confident and in control.

On day two, nature would begin to elbow me out of the way and take command. On day three, I would watch helplessly as the wind swept away all my meticulously laid plans and scattered them over the snow-capped mountain peaks. It's a humbling experience having to accept that you're not as clever as you thought you were. But there's also something deeply satisfying in having to roll with the punches, adapting and reacting as best you can to the constantly changing situation in which you find yourself.

One day, I might be walking under a brilliant blue sky in intense heat, wearing only a sweat-soaked T-shirt while trying to protect myself from sunburn and windburn, and battling the effects of altitude sickness. The next morning, or even later that same day, I could be stumbling over barren, rocky terrain, wearing several layers of high-tech clothing designed to cocoon my frozen, painfully numb body against the raging elements. And then, within minutes, I might be sliding and slipping over ground that had been instantly transformed by torrential rain from thin, dry soil to thick, glutinous mud. In conditions like that, all the anxieties and worries of your 'normal' life seem suddenly petty and mundane in comparison to the more immediate need to push yourself beyond physical exhaustion and take just one more step, and then another.

I already knew before I set out that there have been many deaths on the mountains I was going to be walking in, some of them due to human error, others the result of the capricious whims of nature. I'm not a thrill seeker or an adrenalin junkie. I enjoy physical challenges, but I have no desire to die—particularly not in a way that would, in effect, be at my own hands. And I certainly do not want the last word I ever speak to be 'Oh No!' as I realize, too late, that I've just done something incredibly stupid.

So, although it's almost impossible to eliminate every danger from a physically challenging endeavor, I always try to anticipate and plan for the risks that are potentially involved in the adventures I undertake. And I never forget that if you don't give nature the respect she deserves, she might just turn around and slap you in the face—or worse. It was a lesson that was reinforced many times during my treks in the sacred mountains.

Jainism

Based on a philosophy of nonviolence and the belief that all forms of life are equal and spiritually independent, Jainism is one of the oldest religions in the world.

Although its origins are unknown, it was the state religion of India until the 8th century, when it was replaced by Hinduism and Islam. There are now approximately 4 million followers of Jainism in India, as well as small immigrant communities in various other countries.

The name Jainism is derived from the Sanskrit word meaning 'to conquer' and refers to the battle against bodily pleasures that is undertaken by ascetics.

Even in situations in which the risks are limited, trekking in mountainous regions can be extremely uncomfortable. Like many people who live in the modern, developed world, I rarely experience real inconvenience and discomfort. I'm always irritated by the former, but believe in embracing the latter and learning from it—which was just as well, because I was about to have a learning experience I'm unlikely ever to forget!

As well as doing four treks around four sacred mountains in completely different geographical locations, I wanted to spend at least some time with my family. And I had other work commitments that needed to be honored too. After considering all the logistical and practical factors that had to be taken into account, I decided to do one trek every month between July and October.

The idea of performing a *kora* around a sacred mountain is that you encircle it rather than climb it. In fact, the summit of a sacred mountain is where the gods are believed to reside, so attempting to climb it is considered by local people to be a desecration. But as each of the four mountains I was planning to circumambulate is surrounded by other mountains, even encircling it was going to involve scaling high passes at altitudes that would range from about 3000 m to 5800 m (10,000–19,000 ft) above sea level (ASL).

What also had to be taken into account was the fact that there is no simple mathematical relationship between the distance covered in terms of linear kilometers and the degree of difficulty. Allowing for that, and for the additional time we would need for filming, I reckoned that the shortest trek—52 km (32 miles) around Mount Kailash—would take four days and the longest—240 km (149 miles) around Kawa Karpo—would take twelve.

I had already done several trips with my cameraman, Chad, so I knew he was tough, both mentally and physically. Walking with someone who complained and brought negative energy into the mix would have made everything considerably more difficult than it already was. Interestingly, there were days when Chad struggled and I took everything in my stride; and other days when he would be gliding along while I had to push myself to take every step. It was a good illustration of how psychological factors can be as important as physical factors in any arduous journey. In the event, Chad proved to be an even more resilient, compatible walking partner than I had anticipated, and by the end of the first trek, we both had a better idea of just how far we could push ourselves before we would break.

Some of the stress involved in the motorcycle journeys I did with my brother was due to the ever-present feeling that we had to push on to get to certain places at certain times or to avoid delays that would add to the already substantial costs of the whole venture. This time, there were going to be enough stresses involved in pitting ourselves against the elements without the added pressure of having a tight schedule as far as days spent on the mountain were concerned. So if the guides said a particular trek would take eight days, I would add time for filming and then allow (and budget) for twelve.

The main factors I knew we would also have to take into account would be the altitude and the weather. Although we couldn't do anything to prepare for the former, I partnered with The North Face and they provided me with some incredible kit to help protect us against the latter. Lack of sleep was a recurring theme on all the treks too. Often, it was the intense cold that woke me up: despite sleeping on the best sleeping pad, in the best sleeping bag, in the best tent money could buy, it would sometimes penetrate all the layers, seep into my bones and freeze the blood in every artery and vein in my body.

The most stressful days, however, were the ones when we had to ascend to a high pass. And as every trek involved at least one high pass, altitude sickness was something Chad and I had to learn to deal with.

There's half as much oxygen in the air at 5000 m (16,404 ft) as there is at sea level. Until you become acclimatized, even the slightest physical exertion is really difficult and exhausting. Sometimes, every step you take seems to require an almost super-human effort of willpower and physical strength. Even at 4000 m (13,123 ft) ASL, you wake up after a couple of hours hyperventilating and with a pounding headache. Then there's the wind and the bitterly cold temperature to contend with. In conditions like that, it might take you twelve hours to walk 20 km (12.4 miles). But the good news is that, by the time you've gone up to and over a high pass, you're acclimatized, which makes coming down the other side comparatively easy.

As well as all the practical issues, there were personal ones too. For example, the fact that China is my adopted home, the place of my connection with my wife, and somewhere I feel passionate about made me very anxious to produce a story that I could share with people that would make them to understand why I believe that China has some of the most beautiful landscapes, and remarkable alpine scenery, of any country in the world.

It isn't obligatory to 'get' anything from trekking in the mountains: I'm sure that if 100 people completed the same journey, they would have almost as many different views and opinions about what they had experienced. But because I believe that simply connecting with nature makes you stronger and more confident, I don't think anyone could fail to benefit from it in some way.

My wife and I go traveling every year, usually on a driving trip in China or abroad. Every year, we see different places and have different experiences, but the really important thing about those trips is that we talk. We look forward to spending that time together, just the two of us in a car, talking about our lives and our work

John Muir

In 1849, when John Muir was 11 years old, his family emigrated from Scotland to Wisconsin, in the USA, where his parents became farmers. The strict religious doctrines that had sometimes been beaten into Muir when he was boy were replaced in adulthood by less orthodox beliefs. But he remained a deeply spiritual man.

An interest in the natural world that had begun to develop when Muir was still a boy in Scotland was further fueled by his studies in botany, geology, and chemistry at the University of Wisconsin. When he left university, he worked for a while as a sawyer before completing a 1000-mile walk from Indiana to Florida, which he recounted in a book. After moving to California, where he worked for a season as a shepherd in Yosemite, he spent most of his time hiking and mountain climbing.

Although writing for Muir was a laborious, tiresome effort, he wrote several books, as well as hundreds of papers based on his own extensive geological and botanical studies.

As co-founder and president of the Sierra Club, John Muir played a key role in establishing Yosemite National Park. But he was a preservationist rather than a conservationist, with an unwavering belief in the spiritual powers of nature.

By the time of his death in 1914, the naturalist, author and pioneering preservationist John Muir—'the patron saint of American wilderness'—had been instrumental in changing people's attitude towards the natural world forever.

and making plans for the future. Walking in the mountains has a similar effect for me. I didn't set out on my treks with any idea that I had problems to solve; but without the constant distractions of daily life, I found that I was able to think with real clarity, and by the time I walked down off the fourth sacred mountain, I knew who I was and what I wanted to do.

What follows is the story of four extraordinary journeys that pushed me to the limits of physical endurance, reconnected me with the natural world, replenished my soul, and changed me forever. I hope that when you've read my story, you'll feel inspired to make a journey of your own. It doesn't have to be to some remote region of the world; it doesn't even have to be beyond the borders of your own country to be an epic adventure in its own way. What's important is to do what John Muir was urging people to do more than 100 years ago: '. . . *break clear away, once in awhile, and climb a mountain or spend a week in the woods. Wash your spirit clean.*'

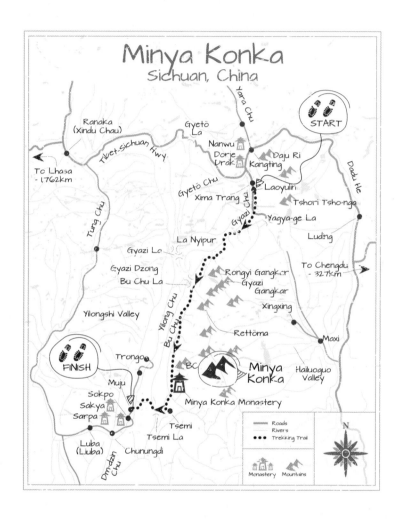

Minya Konka
Sichuan, China

Ranaka
(Xindu Chau)

Gyetö
La

Yara Chu

START

Nanwu
Dorje
Drak

Daju Ri

Tibet-Sichuan Hwy.

Kangting

To Lhasa
- 1,762km

Gyetö Chu

Laoyulin

Xima Trang

Tshori Tsho-nga

Gyozi Chu

Yagya-ge La

Luding

Tung Chu

La Nyipur

Gyazi La

Rongyi Gangkar

To Chengdu
- 327km

Gyazi Dzong
Bu Chu La

Gyazi
Gangkar

Yilong Chu

Xingxing

Yilongshi Valley

Bu Chu

Rettöma

Maxi

FINISH

Trongo

BC

Minya
Konka

Muju

Hailuoguo
Valley

Sokpo
Sakya
Sarpa

Minya Konka Monastery

Luba
(Liuba)

Tsemi

Chunungdi

Tsemi La

Dmdzin Chu

Roads
Rivers
Trekking Trail

N

Monastery   Mountains

Minya Konka

At 7556 m (24,790 ft) above sea level, Minya Konka—known to the Chinese as Gongga Shan—is the highest mountain in Sichuan Province and the third highest outside the Himalayas.

In 1929, when the Austrian-American botanist and explorer Joseph Rock undertook an expedition to Minya Konka, he miscalculated the elevation of the mountain and identified it as the highest in the world —an error that was fortunately rectified before publication by the National Geographic Society.

When Joseph Rock was exploring Asia, the Tibetan Plateau was a dangerous place, controlled by quarrelsome warlords who paid no attention to the ruling emperor in Beijing. But although the historical reputation of Tibetans is as tough, ruthless, warriors and bandits, the Tibetans who live in the shadow of Minya Konka originate from a gentler race of primarily nomadic yak herders.

/ 1 \

Tibetan Buddhists believe that deities inhabit the summits of all the sacred mountains and that merely gazing at the peak of Minya Konka—which some consider to be the most beautiful place on Earth—will wipe away all your sins. Climbing it, however, would be deemed to be sacrilegious—and, from a practical point of view, extremely dangerous, even for an experienced climber.

In terms of number of deaths compared to successful ascents, Minya Konka is amongst the deadliest mountains in the world. Between 1932, when it was scaled for the first time by a small group of American climbers, and 1999, only eight teams—comprising a total of 24 climbers—successfully reached its summit. During that same period, more than 20 people died or went missing on its majestic but merciless peak.

Fortunately, it wasn't my intention to attempt to climb the mountain. What I was planning to do was follow in the footsteps of generations of religious pilgrims and perform a *kora* around it. I was about to discover that cleansing my sins by looking at its snow-capped peak wasn't as easily accomplished as it might sound. In fact, it isn't until you're nearing the end of your journey that you can see the mountain at all, from the narrow valley that stretches beneath the ridge on which the Gongga Monastery stands. And, even then, if the peak of Minya Konka is enshrouded by clouds, as it often is for days on end during the summer months, it's quite possible to complete your *kora* without ever having set eyes on it at all.

Our adventure started on 6th July 2013, when Chad and I flew 1600 km (1000 miles) west from Shanghai to the city of Chengdu—the capital of Sichuan Province and the fourth most populous city in Mainland China.

The flight from Shanghai to Chengdu takes just 2½ hours, but it had been delayed for more than seven hours, so it was 04.00 by the time we checked into our hotel. Just four hours later, we were awake again. After breakfast, we packed up the car we'd hired locally, complete with driver, and were on the road by 11.00, en route to the small mountain town of Kangding, where we would start our trek, approaching the mountain from the south.

Setting out from Chengdu felt like leaving civilization behind. Although the distance between Chengdu and Kangding is only a little over 300 km (186 miles), the increase in elevation is almost 2000 m (6562 ft) and it took us eight hours to get there on roads that twist and turn their way up through the mountains.

Kangding occupies what was once a strategic position on the border between China and Tibet. For many centuries, it was the site of numerous conflicts between the two cultures and an important trading hub, where Chinese block tea was exchanged for Tibetan wool. Today, it has a population of approximately 100,000, comprised primarily of ethnic Tibetans and Han Chinese. For such a small, relatively unimportant town, it's perhaps surprising that almost everyone in China has heard of it—not, as one might imagine because it is the birth place of some important historical, political or media figure, but because of the Kangding Love Song. A traditional folk song that is popular throughout China, the Kangding Love Song has lent its name to almost everything in town, including the hotel where we stayed that night.

July is the height of the summer season and the town was heaving with tourists, including hundreds of cyclists preparing for long rides into the high plateaus of Tibet. (We must have passed at least 1000 cyclists on the road from Chengdu.) Until fairly recently, cycling as a leisure activity wasn't popular in China. In the cities, the wealthy drive large, powerful cars and bicycles are ridden primarily by the less affluent (and very brave). It's a common sight in any Chinese town or city to see bicycles being used to transport entire families or immense loads, precariously stacked and balanced. Outside the cities, however, the country's burgeoning middle classes and increasing number of young, relatively affluent people are beginning to look for adventure. Cycling is just one of the activities that have evolved to accommodate them—partly inspired by the popular film *One Mile Above*.[1]

At Kangding, we met up with our translator, Tersing, who came from Xining in Qinghai Province and whose services I had booked from Shanghai. It had been a tiring drive and the sound of every honking horn in the town increased my longing to be in the mountains. So, after we had checked into the Kangding Love Song Hotel and had something to eat, I went to bed.

From the practical point of view, I was as prepared as I could be for the journey that lay ahead. Sometimes on the motorcycle adventures I had shared with my brother, the problems we encountered made things more interesting. But whereas you can predict a lot of the problems—or types of problems—you're likely to have to deal with on a motorcycle journey, I knew that in the mountains there were likely to be some I hadn't anticipated. For someone who likes to be in control, I was unnerved by the fact that I didn't know how it was all going to play out.

At least I didn't have to worry about Chad: I knew from traveling with him before that he's as tough as nails and that he would get some good film footage come hell or high water. That still left a hundred uncertainties and questions buzzing around in my head like agitated flies. Did we bring enough batteries and memory cards? Would I think of interesting things to say on camera? What would the weather be like during the next few days? Would we spend every day walking in clouds and never actually see the mountains around us, let alone Minya Konka itself? The best time to do the journey we were about to do is between late September and October, although snow can fall on the mountain in any season. Ideally, it's best to avoid the rainy season that falls in the months of June and July. As we were setting out in early July, we were going to be pretty much in the middle of it.

I knew from experience that the night before the first day of a journey is the worst time for doubts and uncertainties. I was ex-

1. *One Mile Above* is the story of a young Taiwanese man who decides to do a trip his brother was planning to do before he was killed in an accident and cycle them from Taiwan to the highest point in Tibet.

Tea in Tibet

Tea is a big thing in Tibet. Wherever there are people, the distinctive odor of yak-butter tea seems to hang in the air. But they like sweet milk tea too, and boiled black tea, green tea, milk tea . . .

Tea lies at the heart of almost every type of traditional Tibetan ceremony and drinking it involves many rules. For example, when being welcomed to someone's home, the host will pour some barley wine, into which the guest must dip a finger before flicking it into the air three times. The host will then present the guest with a glass or bowl of yak-butter tea, which must be accepted without touching the rim. After drinking the tea, the guest must pour another bowl, and drink it all to avoid insulting the host and appearing rude.

---

periencing some minor effects of the increased altitude too, after traveling fairly swiftly from Shanghai at sea level to Kangding at 2415 m (7923 ft). Fortunately, I was so tired by the time we went to bed I think I could have stretched out on the floor and slept for twelve hours.

The next morning, after a bleak breakfast of hard-boiled eggs, congee—a sort of rice porridge—and salted peanuts, we packed up the car and headed south about half and hour's drive to the village of Laoyulin, where we would hire some guides with donkeys to accompany us on our trek. There's no mobile phone connection in the more remote regions of Tibet, and even where there is, most people in the small villages don't have phones. So there's no way of planning the local aspects of a trip until you get to the point of departure—which in our case was the village of Laoyulin itself. From then on, it was all up in the air. If there were a lot of tourists in the region or if the men who act as guides in the summer months were still in the mountains grazing their yaks, there might not be anyone left in the village who could guide us. I had been able to make contact a couple of weeks earlier with a man named Jangbu, a local fixer and guesthouse owner who turned out to be a big, super nice guy with a large, cheerful family. When we arrived in Laoyulin, we headed straight for his stone-built guesthouse with its brightly painted windows, which stands at the edge of the village in a small valley surrounded by mountains. After perform-ing a tea ceremony to welcome us to his home, Jangbu presented each of us with a *khatak*, the white ceremonial scarf that is given to guests in Tibet on arrival or departure and to mark important events such as births and weddings. Then, with the ceremonies complete, we waited at the guesthouse while he went off and found us four guides—including one who had to be fetched down from the mountains where he was herding his yaks. That afternoon, af-ter we had unpacked the car and paid off the driver, we did a short trek into the mountains. Laoyulin is 2954 m (9692 ft) above sea level, and we were going to be going much higher, so I wanted to start the process of acclimatizing our bodies to the altitude and preparing ourselves for the arduous journey that lay ahead. There's good reason why the Tibetan Plateau is sometimes referred to as the roof of the world, and although I was in good physical shape, I knew that walking in the mountains was going to involve using largely untapped reserves of energy and muscles I didn't even know I had. So Chad and I climbed a few small hills behind Jangbu's house—up to about 4000 m (13,123 ft)—and got back in time to have a wash before sitting down for a really great meal of spicy rice, peppers, green cabbage, and potatoes fried in their skins.

If you're lucky, you can sometimes get yak meat, but there's very little of any other type of meat in that part of the world, and with-out the protein, your muscles soon start to break down. You could eat eggs instead, but when you're trekking and all your provisions are being carried by donkeys or yaks, food like eggs and fresh fruit would simply get bruised and crushed. The first time I had done a difficult walk in the mountains—which was in 2007, with my good friend Brandon—we had taken protein bars to supplement what was otherwise a diet of rice and vegetables. For the first couple of days, we ate the bars for lunch and dinner, and by day three our bodies were struggling to deal with all that protein. It began to feel as if the excess was accumulating like rocks in our stomachs, and by the time we did eventually accomplish the incredibly painful process of 'passing it', we realized that protein bars are *not* the way to go. So, this time, we would be taking an ample supply of Snickers bars, peanuts, and dried fruit.

Altitude sickness

The human body works best at sea level, where the concentration of oxygen in the air is just less than 21% and the hemoglobin molecules in the blood, which bind the oxygen and carry it around the body, are saturated. With increasing altitude, the percentage of oxygen in the air remains constant while its atmospheric pressure and partial pressure decrease. It's the partial pressure of oxygen that affects the saturation of hemoglobin, and when it decreases, the blood carries less oxygen and the body has to adapt to compensate.

In terms of mountain medicine, there are basically three main zones related to reduction in oxygen partial pressure: high altitude at 1500–3500 m (4921–11,483 ft); very high altitude at 3500–5500 m (11,483–18,045 ft); and extreme altitude above 5500 m (18,045 ft). Mountaineers add another level above 8000 m (26,247 ft), which they call 'the death zone.'

People differ in their susceptibility to altitude sickness. For most people, it occurs above 2400 m (8000 ft). As the altitude increases, the symptoms become progressively more severe. At 'high altitude', they are relatively nonspecific and similar to those associated with flu or carbon monoxide poisoning. For people who are fit and healthy, acute altitude sickness develops in the 'very high altitude' range and may quickly progress to pulmonary or cerebral edema, which can prove fatal. It is because of the very severe physiological effects at 'extreme altitude' that human beings do not live permanently above 6000 m (19,685 ft) ASL.

I didn't sleep well that night. Although my body was tired, the cogs in my head wouldn't stop turning. I lay awake in my bed, listening to the sound of the rain beating down on the roof above my head and trying to imagine what it would be like to be sleeping in a tent on such a stormy night. It wouldn't be long before I would find out.

We stayed at Jangbu's house for another day, to give ourselves more time to acclimatize and to do some more filming. I didn't sleep any better the next night either, perhaps because I was suffering some minor effects of the altitude, which meant that even tossing and turning in bed left me hyperventilating and out of breath.

On any trek in the mountains, it's important to be aware of the effects and potential dangers of altitude sickness. In the village of Laoyulin, we were in what's known as the 'high altitude' region, and, after a second restless night, there was no comfort to be had from the knowledge that we were about to get much higher.

The morning after our second night at Jangbu's house, we had a really good breakfast of fried eggs and hot, doughy, freshly cooked Tibetan bread, which is the perfect way to fill your stomach on a cold morning. Then we continued our acclimatization program by doing some more light trekking in the hills. It had rained in the night, and the rivers were raging, which was a sobering reminder of the fact that I had chosen to do the trek to Minya Konka during one of the warmest but wettest months of the year. I knew it wasn't ideal to be starting the treks in July. The problem was that I wanted to do all four scared mountain pilgrimages within the same year, which meant starting the first one early enough to be able to finish the last one before the snowstorms came and the high passes become impenetrable. As is so often the case when transposing theory into practice, reality didn't quite match expectations, and doing all four treks in just four months proved, in some respects, to be even more of a challenge than I had anticipated.

What had prompted me to make the decision rather than, say, doing two treks one year and the other two the next, was the filming. I was excited about the prospect of sharing my adventure in the form of a documentary, and I didn't want to end the year with it only half finished. However clear, technicolored, and exciting the vision in my own mind, I know from experience that, unless you're David Attenborough or Bear Grylls, no TV executive is going to be more than politely interested in something they can't see, touch, hear, and smell.

Another reason for the tight schedule was the fact that the work I do involves having lots of fingers in lots of pies. So I was afraid that unless I did all the treks almost back to back, I might end up having to commit to something else, which would mean that by the time I did go back to do the last two treks, the continuity would be lost and it would be much more difficult to create something with the feel of a single project.

We returned to the guesthouse earlier than we had intended that afternoon, forced off the hills by torrential rain. It wasn't the good omen I had been hoping for. What would happen if it rained like that while we were on the mountain, where there was no guesthouse to shelter us from the storm? When I had planned our treks in the mountains, I had opted for what seemed to be the most sensible compromise in terms of time frame. Now, I was beginning to wonder if we would be doing the first trek when it was too wet and the last when it was too cold.

While Chad and I were walking in the hills, getting soaked to the bone and discovering new things to worry about, Tersing had been talking to our guides and buying all the food we were going to need. When we got back to the guesthouse, Chad and I repacked our bags and then had a meeting with Tersing.

Safety factors would overrule any other considerations at all times while we were on the mountain. On subsequent treks, assessing safety issues became an almost subconscious routine, but it was something I did consciously every step of the way on Minya Konka. After safety, what really mattered was the filming, because although the treks we were about to undertake were important to me on a personal level, their primary purpose was work.

When you're spending days in what are sometimes very tough conditions, you *have* to get on with the people you're with. As I was to discover on one of the later trips, when you're soaking wet, freezing cold, exhausted, and stuck on the side of a mountain, even a mildly incompatible companion can become a disproportionately discordant irritation. I had worked with Chad on many occasions in the past, but never in such restrictive circumstances. Fortunately, both he and Tersing proved to be brilliant people to walk with.

It rained heavily throughout our last night at Jangbu's guesthouse, and it was still drizzling in the morning. I wasn't expecting our guides to arrive with their donkeys at 08.00, as we'd arranged—the hands of Tibetan clocks move at a slower pace than the clocks in other parts of the world. And although I'm usually irritated when people are late, I was determined on this occasion to try to relax and adjust my expectations to take account of local time keeping. So I was pleasantly surprised when they turned up at 09.00. It was our first good omen.

An hour later, the six donkeys were loaded and our adventure had begun.

/ 2 \

For the next few days, the role of our English-speaking translator, Tersing, would be crucial. I speak some Chinese—although not as much as I should do after living in China for thirteen years—but I don't understand the Tibetan dialects. So, as well as acting as an interpreter and go-between with our Tibetan guides, Chad and I would need to rely heavily on him to take care of all our film-making, eating, and camping needs. When you're doing something innately stressful that involves trying to focus on a hundred things at the same time, you need to know that the people around you are able to take the initiative and get on with all the basic stuff without constantly asking you questions. Tersing had been recommended to me by a friend of a friend and he turned out to be worthy of his good reputation.

We set out on our first day of walking—which was day four since we had arrived in Chengdu—on a paved road. After an hour or so, we reached a point where the road continued in one direction and the trail we were going to follow branched off south through the narrow Yulin River valley. Once we had left the road, we were on a gravel path that took us up into the forest where the mostly coniferous trees provided little protection from the rain that continued to fall throughout the rest of the day. The trail through the forest followed a gentle incline of about 700 vertical meters and then we were above the tree-line on open grassland, where the vegetation was primarily low-lying shrubs.

However cold you are before you set out, your body warms up pretty quickly when you start walking. But then, once you're warm, you're reluctant to stop for any reason, because you know that if you do, the sweat will cool down almost instantly and suck all the

The Tibetan language

Although there is just one written Tibetan language, there are many regional dialects, some of which are considered by the people who speak them to be completely separate languages, mostly for political reasons.

It is estimated that some form of Tibetan-based language is spoken by approximately eight million people in Nepal, northern India, and Bhutan, as well as across the Tibetan Plateau.

With the dissemination of Tibetan Buddhism, the written language has also spread in recent years to countries in the West, as some students learn to read it in order to be able to translate Buddhist texts and prayers.

heat out of your body. So, apart from stopping for five minutes every hour and a half to eat peanuts and Snickers bars and do some filming, we pushed on relentlessly. Walking for hours without any real breaks is a regime not everyone would be happy with. But it was one of the things Chad and I had discussed and agreed on the previous night, and in any case, he had worked with me before and already knew I didn't do lunch.

Despite having an excellent waterproof jacket with a hood, I was cold and wet by the time we stopped to pitch camp. And then the rain stopped and the sun came out, almost as if it had been waiting for that moment all day. When you've been walking for hours in persistent rain and the sun suddenly breaks through the clouds, it's very tempting to stop whatever you're doing and lie down on the grass to wait for the heat to warm your body and seep into your aching muscles. The first thing we did, however—on that day and on every day that followed—was put up our tents. The sun might be shining now, but it would only take minutes for the clouds to return, bringing with them lashing rain and howling wind. And when that happens, you need some shelter and not to have to become embroiled in a battle with the wind as you struggle to prevent it whisking away your half-pitched tent.

We set our camp that night at 3674 m (12,054 ft). Chad, Tersing, and I had our own tents and the three guides slept together in another one. There was also a fifth, pyramid-shaped, canvas tent, for cooking in and storing all our food overnight. We ate our breakfast in it too, on the mornings when it was raining and cold.

When all the bags had been unloaded, the donkeys had been fed, and the tents were up, we took off all our wet clothes and draped them over rocks to dry them for as long as the sun stayed out, and then ate a very welcome hot meal. Once you get above the tree-line in the mountains, there is no firewood. So, amongst all the other equipment carried by the ever-patient donkeys, were a cooker and two tanks of propane gas. We always brought gas with us, even when there was likely to be wood to collect for fires, because it gave us almost instant and controllable access to boiled water. On a mountain, when your body temperature plummets as soon as you stop walking, you live and die by hot water.

Keeping yourself hydrated is crucial on any trek in the mountains. I always carried a small camelback containing gloves, a sun hat, a winter hat, chocolate bars, and water that I drank through a tube while I was on the move. In reality, however, short of getting a constant supply of fluid through an i.v. tube, it's almost impossible to prevent yourself becoming hydrated when you're walking for maybe eight hours in one day. Fortunately, on this particular day, as soon as we were above the tree-line and beyond the polluting reach of civilization, we were able to fill our camelbacks with clean, cold water from the glacial river.

The one indulgence Chad and I did allow ourselves was to have a cup of powdered Nescafé every morning. Tea and coffee simply add to the problems of dehydration and are best avoided altogether. But sometimes a bit of dehydration seems a small price to pay for a boost that will get you up and on your feet again. In fact, when you're at that sort of altitude, you always wake up dehydrated in the mornings, with chapped lips and an incredibly dry mouth. So the first thing I always did was fill my camelback with a liter of hot water and honey, which I would drink before I had the coffee.

I was doing my video diary that first night when we saw the clouds roll in like billowing smoke from a massive fire, concealing everything in their path and filling the landscape with eerie silence. Then the thunder started. I had never been in the mountains during a full-scale thunderstorm before: it was spectacular. The lightning lit up the sky with the power of a million fluorescent light bulbs as the sound of the thunder bounced off every mountain until it seemed to fill the entire valley. It was a pulse-racing, ear-splitting experience, and at times really quite scary.

At the end of the first day of our *kora* around Minya Konka, I had the same sense I had on the motorcycle journeys of having been severely tested. And I was reminded once again that no matter how meticulously you plan, you don't know what it's actually going to be like until you're doing it.

Chad and I were both suffering from altitude sickness and felt horrible when we went to bed that night. Despite being exhausted, I didn't sleep well again, partly because I found it difficult to get comfortable in my sleeping bag. We had been given some great equipment by North Face, including some really high-quality mummy-shaped sleeping bags—the type that are wide at the shoulders and taper down towards the feet. They're the warmest sleeping bags you can get, which we knew would be an essential attribute in the sort of conditions and temperatures we were going to be sleeping in. The trouble is, once you're zipped inside a mummy bag, your movements are restricted and you have to sleep on your back, which I found a bit claustrophobic until I got used to it.

I had gone to bed with a pounding headache and when I woke up at about 07.00, the intensity of the pounding didn't seem to have lessened at all. I wanted to roll over and go back to sleep, but the first action was prevented by the constrictions of the sleeping bag and the second by the sound of rain beating down on the tent above my head. To make sure the rain hitting your tent runs off rather than pooling on the surface, the material has to be very tightly stretched, and there's nothing like tightly stretched tent material to amplify the sound of the rain that continued to fall throughout the night. As I lay there, I tried to focus on the positives—that I was safe, warm, and dry—and not think about the fact that I was sleep deprived, or that we were about to have to face another day of walking in rain of almost biblical proportions, or that the walls of my tent were shaking violently as though the roaring wind was trying to rip it from its moorings.

After packing up the tents, loading the donkeys, and eating a damp, hurried breakfast, we set off on our second day of walking. We ascended to 4109 m (13,481 ft) ASL that day—well into what's considered to be the high-altitude zone in terms of blood oxygen levels. For a lot of the time we were walking on grassland in low cloud, through grass that was barely visible under a carpet of bright-yellow flowers. We were still following the river, which we had to cross several times, mostly on little rickety bridges that have been constructed by nomadic yak herders or perhaps by some of the many pilgrims who'd already trodden the same well-worn track.

We had just made one of our many river crossings and then walked up and over a small ridge when we saw one of the distinctive yak-hair tents that are home to what local people call the 'black tent nomads.' It was cold and still raining and the smoke billowing out of the hole in the top of the tent evoked instant warmth, hot water, and tea. So we decided to introduce ourselves.

I had been looking forward to the 'sociable' part of our journeys —talking to local people, nomadic herdsmen, and pilgrims—both from a personal point of view and because of the interesting dimension it would add to the filming. And the rugged-faced Tibetan who greeted us was happy to talk. A villager from Laoyulin, he takes his 50 or more yaks into the mountains every summer to graze on the grassland pastures and stays there, with his wife and son, until the snows came.

Known in Tibetan as *drokpa*, which translates as 'high-pasture people', there are estimated to be two million nomads wandering the Tibetan Plateau and Himalaya Mountains that extend across the People's Republic of China, Bhutan, India, and Nepal. While China and most of the rest of the world speed hell-bent towards modernization, the lives of the Tibetan nomads are virtually the same as those of their ancestors stretching back over many generations. All that matters to the *drokpa* are the seasons, the quality of the pastureland, and the births and deaths of their animals. And because the Tibetan culture has its roots in a nomadic existence, Tibetans are renowned for their hospitality to strangers.

The man and his wife and son were friendly and offered us tea

Tsampa

Barley is one of the few crops that will grow at the high altitude of the Tibetan Plateau. Tsampa is roasted barley flour, which is commonly mixed with yak-butter tea or eaten as porridge and is a staple food in Tibet.

To make tsampa, you put a small amount of yak-butter tea in a bowl (water or even beer is sometimes used instead of tea), add a generous amount of barley flour, and stir with your forefinger. Then, while turning the bowl continuously, you work the mixture with your hand until it resembles a large lump of dough or a dumpling.

It takes a lot of practice to acquire the manual dexterity and the ability to judge the correct proportions of tea to flour that are essential to the whole operation.

The finished product is bland and filling and is usually washed down with copious amounts of tea.

and *tsampa* made from yak butter, yak cheese, sugar, barley wheat, and tea. Making *tsampa* is quite a skill, as I discovered when I tried to do it myself. Resting the palm of your hand against the outer surface of the bowl, you use your index and middle fingers to mix the tea into the other ingredients until it forms an almost solid block resembling uncooked pastry or bread dough—which, in effect, is what it actually is.

Much to the amusement of the whole family, I clearly don't have the dexterity the process requires. And then it was my turn to laugh when, after trying to teach me how to do it, the guy announced solemnly, 'You are not good at this.'

When your lifestyle involves being constantly on the move and you have to carry all your worldly possessions with you, you find that you don't need much. At least, that's what you would think. Inside the tent there was a wooden-slatted bed for the husband and wife, another for the child, a small, yak-dung-fueled stove under a pipe that collected most of the smoke and exhaled it into the atmosphere through a hole in the top of the tent, an assortment of prayer wheels, framed pictures of family members and Buddhist monks . . . there was stuff everywhere. And outside there were

Yaks

Yaks are well adapted to living in mountain terrain. In addition to having an ability to conserve their body heat, which enables them to survive at very low temperatures, they can also tolerate the high levels of solar radiation found in the mountains.

Yaks are adapted to living in the low oxygen pressures found at altitude by having hemoglobin with an unusually high affinity for oxygen, large lungs, and a massive heart.

Yaks have many uses in the mountain regions of Tibet. As well as being pack animals, they are a source of dung for fuel, fiber for cloth, meat, and milk.

portable solar panels to power the TV that was kept in a sort of briefcase.

It was still raining when we left the family and followed the river up and over a ridge into a valley and another expanse of grassland. Despite the weather, we made good progress that day, and were rewarded by being able to camp for the night in a spectacular grassland amphitheater with a cast of grazing yaks surrounded by breathtakingly beautiful, snow-covered mountains.

The ground was wet, and at that altitude wet means cold. But the rain stopped for a while and as I peeled off layer after soggy layer of clothing, steam rose off my body like smoke. On the brief occasions when there was a gap in the clouds, the tops of the mountains were instantly bathed in brilliant golden light that made the yellow petals of the flowers on the grassland shrugs appear to be made of sunlight.

It was only 14.30 when we stopped walking for the day, and after we had put up our tents, I went over to talk to some nomads who were camped nearby. When someone suggested I should help our neighbor feed his yaks, I quashed my instinctive wariness and decided I needed to think like a film producer.

Yaks are strong, massive creatures that would probably come off best in a confrontation with almost any other animal. So although the young ones have to be corralled at night to protect them from the many wolves that roam the mountainsides, the adults can be left to wander freely. I would often hear them snorting and sniffing outside our tents in the darkness—looking for vegetable matter to eat, I was assured, not human flesh! In fact though, my real concern whenever I was woken up in the night by one of them brushing against the side of my tent was that if it did stumble and accidentally place a hoof on my hand or leg, the journey would be over.

What the herdsman really wanted help with was the process of rounding up the young yaks, one by one, and putting them into a tent for the night. Like any mothers, yaks don't like to be separated from their young, and while the man spirited away their offspring, it was my allocated job to distract them by offering them salt on my outstretched hand.

I think I've already mentioned that I have a healthy respect for wild animals—and for most domestic ones, too, if I'm being totally honest. While being eager to help, I was wary of playing a part in any scenario involving huge—and by now very suspicious—beasts with massive pointed horns. When the mother yaks realized what was going on, would they go for the guy who was shepherding away their young or for the one who'd deliberately diverted their attention so that the dastardly deed could be done?

I had read somewhere that yaks live in large herds to protect themselves against attacks by wild animals, and that they're nervous of humans and will flee if they're startled. I don't know if the person who wrote those words had ever actually witnessed the reaction of a startled yak, because the colossal beasts that were heading directly for me, looking very much like bulls in sheep's clothing, didn't seem to be on the verge of running away.

'It's no big deal,' Tersing told me when I hesitated and took several stumbling steps backwards. 'Yaks don't have teeth. They'll just lick the salt off your hand.' Perhaps something got lost in translation, because these animals certainly appeared to have teeth. In fact, looking into the open mouth of the one nearest to me was like looking into a dark, cavernous graveyard full of huge tombstones. In my panic, I dropped the salt on the ground and, taking a leaf out of the little-read yak-behavior manual, turned and fled.

Day six of our journey to the sacred mountain of Minya Konka was one of the few really stressful days of the trek. Usually, it didn't

> ## Mountain passes
>
> A mountain pass is a route over the ridge of a mountain or through a mountain range that makes use of a natural geographical gap or col. It is often the highest point—and the only level ground—between two valleys, just above the source of a river. A pass can be short and accessed only via steep slopes, or a long valley extending for several kilometers.
>
> Topographically, mountain passes are identifiable on maps as areas where the contour lines are hour-glass shaped, indicating a low point between two higher ones.
>
> Historically, mountain passes have played an important role in the establishment of trade routes, in conflicts between tribes and nations, in cultural exchanges, migration, and the mixing of races.

really matter where we camped as long as it was somewhere safe and relatively protected from the elements. Unlike the motorcycle journeys, we didn't have to reach any specific destination on any particular day. So, if the weather was bad and the path was grueling, we could afford to take our time. The only thing that really mattered was that we didn't press on too long and end up walking in the dark.

I had slept well the night before. When I woke up, it was still raining. The typical morning scene that was developing on this trip would include me standing in the rain with my shoulders hunched, wearing six layers of clothing, my face hidden under the hood of my jacket, with my cold hands curled around a plastic bottle full of coffee.

That morning, within 20 minutes of having packed everything up and started walking, the rain stopped, the clouds dispersed and the sun came out. When that happens, it changes everything. Feeling the warmth of the sun on your skin alters your whole mentality and suddenly you feel positive about whatever the day holds for you.

We set out across gently inclining grassland that gradually became rockier and more barren until all traces of greenery had disappeared and any ground that wasn't covered by huge, flat, shiny slabs of granite had turned to friable grey dust. As the land around us began to resemble the surface of the moon, I put my sun hat in my camelback and took out my winter hat and gloves. By this time, we were heading almost straight up towards Bu Chu La (*La* means pass in Tibetan) at 4816 m (15,800 ft) and as the walking became more challenging, I found it increasingly difficult to breathe.

Walking at that sort of altitude, you run the risk of getting severely sunburned, even when it's cloudy, and on that particular day there wasn't a single cloud in the sky. We had put on sunscreen in the morning, but I still got cooked, and burned by the wind too.

Walking in the mountains at any significant altitude involves few moments of physical comfort. When you're 5000 m (16,400 ft) or more closer to the sun than you are when you're by the sea and there are no clouds to filter its fierce heat, you feel as though you're being roasted alive. When the clouds roll in, they're going to dump either rain or snow on you, and then you're going to be wet and cold. In both scenarios, there's likely to be wind as well. There's enormous satisfaction to be gained from trekking in the mountains and, when the clouds disperse, the views are indescribably beautiful.

Reaching the high pass after walking for five hours felt like a huge achievement. Perhaps it's always the case that the more difficult the journey, the more satisfying the arrival. The view in every direction was spectacular. Behind us was the sun-scorched, barren terrain we had just traversed. Ahead of us was the lush, flower-carpeted Moxi Valley.

We were elated to have made it to the first high pass of our first trek. And it was because of our excitement and our desire to film our surroundings from every possible angle that we made a rookie mistake and stayed up there for too long. Like Icarus, we had ventured too close to the sun; but instead of melted wings, I suffered severe sunburn and windburn on every single exposed part of my body, including my eyes after I stupidly took off my sunglasses while we were filming.

We must have stayed up at the high pass for about an hour before we began the descent into the Moxi Valley. Contrary to what you might expect, walking down a mountain is even more difficult and more painful than going up it. Already exhausted by the ascent, it feels as though the air supply to your lungs has been cut off, and it isn't long before every joint in your body is aching. You get used to it though, as I was to discover on the subsequent treks. Or, at least, you learn that if you focus on pushing through the pain and the almost incapacitating weariness, you'll eventually come out the other side, tired but triumphant.

We camped that night at 4007 m (13,146 ft), in a grassy field next to a stone shelter that must have been built many years ago by nomadic herdsmen to protect themselves from the wind while they slept. It took us two hours every morning to take down the tents and pack everything up, and two hours every evening to reverse the process, which adds another four hours to a day when you've walked for at least eight.

After our first really difficult day, I didn't even have enough energy left to eat. So at about 7.30, after I'd done my video diary, I filled my drinking bottle with hot water, crawled into my tent, and slept like a baby for the next nine hours.

It's interesting how a good long sleep can be a complete game changer: you go to bed shattered, with your spirits at rock bottom, and wake up feeling cheerful and ready to take on the world. In fact, euphoric highs followed by despairing lows were a feature of all the treks. The key to surviving them is to remember that, as with mountain trekking itself, every down will eventually be followed by an up.

/ 3 \

When I woke up on day seven—feeling slightly disorientated after having had the deepest, best sleep of the entire trip—I had a vague sense that something was wrong. I had been standing outside my tent surveying the early-morning landscape for several seconds before it finally dawned on me that I couldn't hear the clinking of the bells the donkeys wore around their necks. Normally, the donkeys would have been sniffing around the tents, eating grass and chewing small shrubs. That morning, there wasn't a single one to be seen.

Tersing and the guides didn't seem to be particularly concerned about the absence of the donkeys. But when they didn't find any of them on the other side of the hill behind the tents, where they thought they would be, it was agreed that Chad, Tersing, and I would pack up the camp while the guides went off to look for the animals.

The guides left at 09.00, two of them heading off in one direction, two in another, and for the rest of the day we just sat there, waiting, writing in our diaries, and chatting about what had happened on the trip so far. As the hours slipped by and the guides still didn't return, we became increasingly concerned that something might have happened to them and/or to the donkeys. Eventually, we agreed that if they hadn't returned by 14.00, we would stay at the same campsite for a second night. At 1.30, we pitched our tents again and accepted the fact that we weren't going anywhere that day.

The guides were local to the region and had been walking in these same mountains since they were children. So the one positive was that, as they had split up and gone in different directions, it was unlikely that anything untoward had happened to all four of them.

After we had re-set our camp, I dozed for a while and then passed some time washing in the river that flowed near our camp-site. On a long, strenuous trek, keeping yourself clean serves the dual purpose of raising your morale at the same time as reducing your unpleasant personal odor. The problem is that, even in July, the glacial river water is icy cold, so you tend not to wash as often as you should. (If there isn't an ancient proverb that says 'If you want to know how difficult someone's journey has been, look at the dirt on their pants,' then there should be!) But when the sun's out, it's nice to swim in a river and then wash in the water before drying yourself off—very quickly—and putting on a fresh pair of socks and underwear. It's often the simple things that make you feel good, and swimming in the river that day helped to rejuvenate my weary muscles and heal the aches and pains that seemed to afflict almost every part of my body.

It was 16.00 by the time the guides came back with the don-keys. Apparently, when they picked up their trail, they also saw the tracks of wolves that must have come into the camp during the night looking for food. Fortunately, the donkeys had stayed together when they ran off, so none of them had been hurt by the pursuing wolves, which, as well as being a relief to the guides, was compensation for their otherwise wasted day.

Things turned out well for all of us in the end. We had too many bags to be able to walk even 100 steps without the donkeys, so Chad and I had been forced to take an unscheduled rest day. Nor-mally, I would have been in a state of high tension after having done nothing for an entire day. But it gave us the opportunity to recover from the previous day's exertions.

We hadn't actually planned to have *any* rest days on the first trek. Not because timing was an issue, but for the same reason we didn't usually stop for lunch. After you've been walking for a while, you get into a rhythm; if you stop, you break it and have to re-establish it when you start to walk again. And perhaps the rest day was also good for Tersing too, although he didn't ever show

Minya Konka. I have my picture taken with Jangbu's family outside his guest-house in Laoyulin, where we stayed before setting out on our trek.

Minya Konka. Following the river south from Laoyulin up into the mountains.

Minya Konka. Yaks graze amongst the yellow flowers that cover the grassland outside my tent in the early-morning sunshine.

Minya Konka. The green grasslands give way to brown dust as we reach the high plateau of southern Sichuan Province.

Minya Konka. A male yak with large horns attacked one of our donkeys, leaving it with a severe leg wound—just one example of the many risks of trekking on the high plateau.

Minya Konka. As we follow the Moxi River down the lush, fertile Moxi Valley, we are just a few days away from our first sighting of the sacred mountain.

Minya Konka. Another camp site amongst the flowers, this time in the late afternoon in the Moxi Valley.

Minya Konka. In the distance, beyond the red rooftops of the Gongga Monastery, is the snow-streaked peak of Minya Konka.

Minya Konka. The sacred mountain is framed by prayer flags in the grounds of the Gongga Monastery.

Amne Machin. Dark clouds gather above the gates that mark the start of the trek near the village of Xiadawu.

Amne Machin. Brilliant blue sky throws the topography into sharp relief on the high grassland plateau that makes up much of southern Qinghai Province.

Amne Machin. A triangular patch of red prayer flags resembles a field of poppies on a slope above a monastery on the outskirts of the village of Xiadawu.

Amne Machin. Under a cloudless sky, two pilgrims do prostrations in the early stages of a journey around the mountain that will take them several weeks to complete.

Amne Machin. Grass has given way to barren, friable dirt and snow-covered rocks as we approach the first high pass of our trek around the mountain.

Amne Machin. The yaks below me in the distance are drinking from what remains of the river on the remote southwestern edge of the mountain.

Amne Machin. The snow-capped peak of the sacred mountain is reflected in the icy water of a small glacial pond.

Amne Machin. We set our camp just in time before dark clouds rolled in to cover the mountains that surrounded us.

Mount Kailash. Potala Palace, on the western edge of the city of Lhasa, is now a museum and World Heritage Site.

Mount Kailash. Looking out from the Drepung Monastery towards western Lhasa and the mountains beyond.

Mount Kailash. An elderly pilgrim spins a prayer wheel as she performs a *kora* around the Jokhang Monastery on Barkhor Square in central Lhasa.

Mount Kailash. Lake Manasarovar—seen here from the Chiu Monastery—is a large freshwater lake south of Mount Kailash and some 15,060 ft (4590 m) above sea level.

Mount Kailash. A bleak campsite on the high-plateau grasslands near the village of Darchen where we stayed prior to setting out on our trek around the most sacred of all the mountains.

Mount Kailash. Our first view of the distant, snow-covered, dome-shaped peak of the sacred mountain. Where else would the gods choose to live?

Mount Kailash. A plethora of prayer flags are suspended from poles and strewn across the rocks at the start of the trek. Mount Kailash is the snow-capped peak on the left in this photograph.

any signs of needing to rest: throughout the entire trek, his energy levels remained consistently high and his good humor never failed.

It was always cold when we woke up in the mornings and as walking was the only way to get warm, particularly before the sun rose above the mountains, I was usually keen to get going. It was damp, cold, and misty that morning, which made packing up the tents a miserable experience. Then we ate our breakfast sitting together, shivering, in a little stone shelter that had been built by nomads at some time in the long-forgotten past.

We had bought all the food for our dinners locally in Laoyulin, so that the guides would be familiar with it and know how to cook it. I had also brought with me from Shanghai the instant coffee, honey, bags of muesli, oatmeal, and raisins Chad and I ate for breakfast every morning. It had added to the already substantial excess-baggage fees I had to pay for all the tents, camera equipment, etc., but it was worth it. I don't know of anything better than sweet, hot oats and coffee to give you the energy you need to get moving on a cold, damp morning. Apart from some nuts and Snickers chocolate bars, it would be the last thing we would eat before dinner that evening.

Prior to setting out on day eight (day five since we had starting walking), I made it clear to everyone that we weren't trying to make up for the day we had lost. Chad and I would spend as much time filming as we would have done before the delay, and the guides should aim to make camp wherever they would have done had everything gone according to the original plan.

Every day, the guides had in their minds two or three different places where we could camp, depending on our rate of progress. Throughout all four treks, there was only ever any stress about reaching a particular point on the days that involved high passes. On those days, we had to ascend to the mountain pass, get through it, and then come down on the other side to a comfortable altitude before it got dark.

After we had been walking for about 20 minutes, the blood started flowing again in my extremities, bringing the feeling back to my toes and fingers. An hour later, I was peeling off layers of clothing and at last my mind could stop focusing on my body and start taking in the surroundings.

We crossed a lot of rivers—sometimes repeatedly—during all the treks. Often, they were small and we could jump across them from rock to rock. Sometimes, as on day eight of the trek around Minya Konka, we encountered the other sort of river—the sort that roars and tumbles down the side of the mountain in a swirling mass of foam. The only way to cross a river like that is to take off your boots, socks, and pants and wade across it, very cautiously.

On our first treacherous crossing that day, despite being less than a meter deep, the force of the water was almost enough to unbalance and knock me off my numb, frozen feet. I realized—as I was slipping and sliding, cutting the soles of my feet on the sharp rocks that lined the riverbed—that it would have been better to have kept my boots on. But it was too late to turn back; all I could do was plant my feet as firmly as possible, shoulder-width apart, bend my knees, face upriver, and push against the current, first with my right leg, then my left.

It took me at least ten minutes to cross that river and I was grateful when Tersing held out his hand to steady me for the last few steps. It was a scary experience, in what otherwise proved to be a successful day.

We traveled a long way that day, mostly on fairly flat ground, through the lush Moxi Valley, past abandoned stone houses that had been built as shelter by seasonal nomads. And we still arrived at the guides' chosen campsite early enough to set up the tents and then sit in the sun while we ate our dinner.

I went to bed that night feeling really positive. For some reason, once I was alone in my tent, I began to worry: 'What am I doing? This is really hard. And after this, I've got to do three potentially even more difficult treks around three more mountains.' Once the anxious thoughts had seduced their way into my brain, I couldn't get rid of them. I lay awake long into the night, thinking about the busy schedule I would be returning to. Over the next few weeks, my time was going to be divided between flying to and from the US to deal with business and family matters and trips and trekking in the mountains.

I was tired and thinking about it all was making me feel mildly panic-stricken. Had I taken on too much this time? In some ways, it might have been easier to do all four mountain treks back to back. Although I knew that wouldn't really have been physically possible, I knew too that every time I went back to my family, it was going to be even more of an emotional wrench to have to leave them again.

On our long motorcycle journeys, my brother and I had been able to fool ourselves repeatedly that *this* was the hardest bit and what lay ahead would be much easier. This time though, I knew that every mountain would present me with a completely new set of challenges. Although I would be fitter after this first trek and might, on subsequent ones, be able to adapt more easily to walking at high altitude, in all other respects I would be starting again.

The next day we were going to visit the Gongga Monastery, from where, weather permitting, we hoped to be able to see the peak of Minya Konka itself for the first time. It was the same on all four treks: for most of the time, you can't actually see the sacred mountain you're encircling, and there's a good chance you won't see it at all if the clouds don't lift at the opportune moment. The day after our visit to the monastery, we would walk over the mountain to the road, where we would be picked up and driven back to 'civilization', and our journey would be over.

Later, on the second mountain and increasingly on the ones after that, I began to have a sense that I was having an extraordinary experience that would affect me in many different ways, perhaps for the rest of my life. That night on Minya Konka, however, I lay awake in my tent, exhausted, worrying, and too tired to be able to think positively about anything.

I woke up on the morning of day nine feeling much more optimistic. It was going to be a short day as far as walking was concerned, with a total change in altitude of just 11 m (36 ft)—from 3611 m to 3600 m (11,847 to 11,811 ft). Chad, Tersing, and I set out ahead of our guides, who were considerably fitter than we were and who always caught us up. They had told us that the route was simple: all we had to do was stay on the trail until we saw the monastery. In fact, it turned out to be quite a nasty journey.

We were walking in mud for most of the day, which was something we hadn't really experienced before. However much it rains at high altitude, the ground remains frozen, so water doesn't really penetrate it. At lower altitudes, the rain turns the ground into a slippery, muddy quagmire that makes walking both hazardous and incredibly tiring.

On the plus side, because we were at a lower altitude, we could walk at a quicker pace and it only took us four hours to reach Gongga Monastery, where we were going to sleep for the night in real beds with a proper, solid roof over our heads. By the time we got there, the day had changed—as it so often did—from miserably cold and wet to sunny and hot. When we reached the monastery, I lay down on the ground in the warm sunshine and fell instantly into a deep sleep. I must have slept for about an hour before I was woken up by the arrival of our guides and the donkeys.

The approach to the monastery was marked by prayer flags, which were flapping noisily in what was now a pleasantly warm breeze. We didn't see as many prayer flags on this trip as we did on all the subsequent ones, and although we had encountered several nomads grazing their yaks, we hadn't met any pilgrims either. There's too much work to be done on the farms and herding animals in the summer months for local people to be able to spare the time for pilgrimages.

Gongga Monastery belongs to a sect of Tibetan Buddhist monks called the Kagyu (Black Hat). Having been badly damaged during China's Cultural Revolution, it has since been repaired. The monastery itself is a four-sided stone building with a red tin roof and brightly painted wooden architrave framing its doors and windows, built around a central courtyard and standing next to a Buddhist temple. Often cut off for up to six months of the year by heavy snowfall, its only inhabitants on the day we visited it were five monks, who offer basic accommodation to pilgrims and travelers like us. After we had unloaded all our bags off the donkeys, we were allocated rooms and I rolled out my sleeping bag on top of a clean bed surrounded by four solid walls and a roof.

The main reason I had wanted to stay at Gongga Monastery wasn't simply because it would make a nice change from sleeping in a tent in sub-zero temperatures. I had been told that the view it affords of the west face of Minya Konka is stunning. However, there was nothing to be seen that night other than thick cloud, which can apparently obscure the mountain for several days at that time of year. We would just have to wait and see what the morning brought.

I slept well that night, until I was woken by my alarm at 05.00. It was hard to leave the warm comfort of the bed, but there was a mountain to film and photograph. At least, I hoped there was.

When I opened my bedroom window at 05.10, I saw a view that, quite literally, took my breath away. There seemed to be a fire burning in the sky and as it turned slowly from brilliant red to pale golden-pink, the clouds cleared to reveal the snow-encrusted peak of Minya Konka. On the journey that had brought us to Gongga Monastery, we had seen several other mountains in the Daxue range. Many of them were so spectacularly beautiful it was hard to imagine that Minya Konka could be 'better' in any way. When you see it, like a massive stone arrowhead pointing to the heavens where the gods reside, you understand immediately why people call it 'the King of Sichuan mountains.'

The monks told us later that it was rare to see Minya Konka without any clouds in the summer. Perhaps the exhaustion and exertions of the last nine days had earned us some good karma. If so, the gods continued to smile on us, because the sky remained cloudless for the rest of the morning. After shooting roll after roll of film, I did a *kora* around the monastery and then went up on the ridge behind it to take some more photographs.

Later, as the clouds rolled in like curtains closing on a stage and concealed the mountain again, I did something all visitors to the monastery should do: I swam in the sacred water of the Minya Konka River.

The young monk who did the cooking at the monastery led us down to the river along a steep, twisting, switchback path lined on either side by hundreds of brightly colored prayer flags. It was about a 30-minute walk and we were still quite some distance away from the river when every other sound was gradually drowned out by the roar of its turbulent waters. Suddenly, even bathing in the calmer pools amongst the rocks didn't seem like such a great idea after all.

As I stood beside the river and took off my clothes, the cool breeze sent a chill through my body and I began to shiver. The monk who'd shown us the way, and who was now sitting peacefully on a rock washing his face and feet, glanced towards me, clearly wondering if I was going to be able to summon up the courage to plunge into the freezing water. But it wasn't his apparent skepticism that spurred me on. I hadn't come all that way only to chicken out at the last minute and miss what might be the only opportunity I would ever have of immersing my already frozen body in the sacred water that flows from the glacier of Minya Konka itself.

There would be no plunging involved, however. Wearing only my underwear—and after several false starts—I eased myself slowly, painfully, and with quite vociferously into the icy water. For a moment, before burning pain spread throughout my body, it felt as though I was being stabbed by a thousand red-hot needles. I submerged myself, very briefly, twice. Then I stood up, stepped out on to the bank and—much to the surprised amusement of the quiet monk—began to jump up and down, waving my arms above my head like the sails of a supercharged windmill as I tried to force blood back into my fingers.

Had immersing myself in the waters of the Minya Konka River left me feeling spiritual in some way? The answer was 'Not really.' But I did feel that I had earned the rest of the afternoon off, and I spent it looking round the monastery, dozing, and writing in my journal.

I went to bed that night feeling very positive. We had survived the trek without any major mishaps, and we had seen the elusive sacred mountain. The high pass hadn't been as high as some we were going to have to traverse on subsequent treks. It had, however, been high enough to make it feel as though we had achieved something worthwhile. Now all we had to do was walk for one more day down through the valley to the road.

I slept well and woke up the next morning—July 16th—to the sound of heavy rain falling like metal pellets on the tin roof of the monastery. We had a long day ahead of us, which I knew would become even longer if the rain continued. Somehow, it didn't seem like a good omen. But by the time our bags were packed, the donkeys were loaded, and we had eaten our breakfast, the rain had stopped, the sun was shining, and the day started to seem manageable after all.

After saying goodbye to the monks, we set off on the long walk that would take us back down to the river before ascending again to the Yulongxi Pass at 4300 m (14,108 ft) and then making our final descent into the Yulongxi Valley. As enjoyable as it was to have had a rest day, I was happy to be on the move again.

It took us nearly two hours to descend to the river, by which time the temperature was rising rapidly and everything I was wearing was damp with sweat. It was good to be walking in warm sunshine rather than bone-chilling rain, even though the ascent that lay ahead of us would be hard work in the heat.

Having crossed a beautiful old wooden bridge that spanned the Moxi River, we started our ascent and soon left the trees behind us. When we eventually stopped to eat some apples and bread, my clothes were sodden and I felt like a partially cooked, boil-in-the-bag fillet of fish. It was windy now that we had left the shelter of the valley, and when I took of my clothes and spread them out on the rocks, they dried quite quickly. The food hit the spot too, and when we set off again I could feel my optimism returning.

The vertical distance between the river and the high pass was about 1000 m (3281 ft). For the next couple of hours after our brief lunch break, the walking was hard and the path was very steep. I was just beginning to feel the effects of the higher altitude when the brilliant blue sky filled with dark clouds. Within seconds, the rain came, followed swiftly by thunder and lightning. There is no positive aspect to being on a mountain at a high altitude without any shelter from the wind and driving rain. When you add into the mix a whiteout and a thunderstorm, the situation has the potential to become extremely dangerous.

We stopped at one point to talk to our guides about the rapidly worsening situation. Should we set our tents and wait for the storm to pass? Or should we push on, even though we could barely see the steep, uneven ground on which we were walking? We didn't need to set the tents, the guides told us; we would just put up an umbrella. When I asked them in what way standing under an umbrella would be better than continuing to walk—either towards the high pass or back down the way we had come—they shrugged. It wasn't the first time I'd had an interesting encounter with Tibetan logic!

The mud itself wasn't too much of a problem: although we couldn't see anything around us, we *could* still see where we were placing our feet. And, in any case, the guides had done this trek so many times they could have carried on blindfolded. What I *was* concerned about, though, was the lightning, particularly in view of the fact that one of our donkeys was carrying two metal containers of propane gas. If a lightning bolt hit the ground close to where that particular donkey happened to be standing, would the gas canisters—and the donkey itself—explode, thereby possibly wiping out anyone who happened to be nearby? As unlikely a scenario as we all agreed that was, I noticed that, after our discussion, everyone—including some of the other donkeys—seemed to be giving the propane donkey a wide berth!

We had been walking for hours by the time we made it to the high pass. Having started the day in sweltering, sweat-inducing heat, even the several layers of clothing I was now wearing weren't enough to keep out the chill of the freezing rain that was being driven into my face by the inexorable wind. It was the worst experience of the whole trip—nature's way, perhaps, of reminding us, before we left the mountain, that we were not the ones who were in charge.

At times like that, all you can really do is keep walking, and eventually you'll get to where you want to go. So that's what I did: I put my head down and focused my mind on my feet. By the time we reached the Yulongxi Valley, I was cold, wet, exhausted, and elated by our achievement.

That night, after we parted ways with our guides, I sat on a little stool beside the road to record my video diary. Then I limped back to the small village guesthouse. The following morning, we hired a car with a driver to take Chad, Tersing, and me back to Kangding, where we said goodbye to Tersing, stayed another night at the Kangding Love Song Hotel, and then drove 40 km to Kang-ding Airport—the third highest airport in the world at 4274 m (14,022 ft) ASL—to board a flight home to Shanghai.

A few months earlier, when I was planning the treks in the sacred mountains, I had many moments of anxiety, wondering if I was taking on more than I could deal with. Would we all complete the journeys safely, without any major mishaps? Would the rain be so relentless and the clouds so persistent that we didn't ever see the sacred mountains themselves—or any of the other mountains that surrounded us as we walked? Would we end up with hours of film footage consisting of me standing in a whiteout, stuttering and stumbling as I tried to think of something interesting to say about the invisible landscape behind me? Was I about to waste a substantial amount of money—my own as well as that provided by the companies that had put their faith in me and provided me with sponsorship?

Now, nearly two weeks after Chad and I had left Shanghai to fly across China, I'd had an incredible adventure in a stunningly beautiful natural wilderness; I had seen the sacred mountain of Minya Konka; and I had the satisfaction of knowing that, even when the going gets tough, I can complete the task I've set myself. And that's a great feeling.

Keep close to Nature's heart . . . break clear away, once in awhile, and climb a mountain or spend a week in the woods. Wash your spirit clean. [JOHN MUIR]

I don't think the true extent of what I had done really sank in until I was back in Shanghai and started going through all the photographs I'd taken and the film footage Chad had shot. During the journey itself, you don't have the time or the energy to think about the context of what you're doing. You live from one moment to the next and focus your attention on dealing with each new physical and mental challenge that arises. It's only later, when you've had a hot shower and have slept for at least one night in a house, in a bedroom, on a clean cotton sheet stretched tightly over a thick sprung mattress, that you might think, 'I did something incredibly rewarding.'

It isn't long before real life takes over again and you resume your roles as husband and father. You drive the kids to soccer or tennis practice, eat regular meals, take care of whatever domestic matters have to be dealt with, and pick up the strands of your work. In my case, that included trying to sort out the logistics and practicalities of my next journey to the sacred mountains of China.

On my secular *kora* around Minya Konka, I had lost almost 7 kg (15 lb) in weight and a lot of muscle mass. We had averaged approximately 15–20 km (9–12 miles) per day—that's a quick pace on land that is neither flat nor at sea level, which isn't bad going. And we had got some really good film footage. In a little over two weeks' time, I would be setting out again to circumambulate a different mountain, in a different geographical location, with what was likely to be a different set of challenges to overcome. I just hoped the confidence I had gained as a result of what I felt I had already achieved wouldn't prove to be unfounded.

The best months to travel to Minya Konka are September and October.

The trek around the mountain begins in the picturesque town of Kangding, sitting at 2560m (8400 ft) above sea level. Be sure to spend a night in Kangding to give yourself some time to acclimatize to the altitude before continuing south to the small Tibetan village of Laoyulin beyond New Kangding. There, amongst the stone houses 'at the end of the road', you will find guides with donkeys to accompany you on your expedition.

It will take 7–9 days to complete your trek around the mountain. In the village of Yulongxi, where your journey ends, you can hire a driver and vehicle for the 8-hour drive back to Kangding. From Kangding, you can travel to Chengdu by plane, bus or private car.

How to Get to Minya Konka

Fly to Chengdu Shuangliu International Airport in Sichuan Province, China.

Either drive southwest for 6 hours or take a 30-minute onward flight from Chengdu to Kangding. While you are in Kangding, be sure to stock up on food at the local markets.

From Kangding, take a taxi south, past New Kangding to the village of Laoyulin at the end of the road, where you will be able to hire a cook and trekking guides with donkeys.

Potential Costs

The following costs are based on the assumption that you are traveling alone, not in a tour group, and were correct in October 2013, when US$ 1 = 6.15 Yuan.

Cost of hiring a car and driver from Chengdu to Kangding: 1500 Yuan. (The flight from Chengdu to Kangding will cost about the same, but I would advise doing this journey by road to help with the acclimatization process.)

Cost per donkey: 150 Yuan per day

Cost per donkey handler/guide/cook: 100 Yuan per day

Cost of food: budget for 200 Yuan per person per day

Car hire from Yulongxi to Kangding: 700 Yuan

Flight from Kangding to Chengdu: 1500 Yuan

Note. Costs might fluctuate during high season. Expect to pay more with a tour group.

How I Completed this Trek

I flew from Shanghai to Chengdu,where I hired a driver and car for
the drive from Chengdu to Kangding.

In Kangding, I hired 1 cook and 2 guides with 7 donkeys.

At the end of the trek, I hired a private van with driver for the drive
from Yulongxi to Kangding, then flew from Kangding to Chengdu
and from Chengdu to Shanghai.

Important note. You should be sure to consult a physician before
attempting any high-altitude trekking. Many pilgrims and travelers
to these regions die each year because of health problems and lack
of preparedness. The risks are REAL.

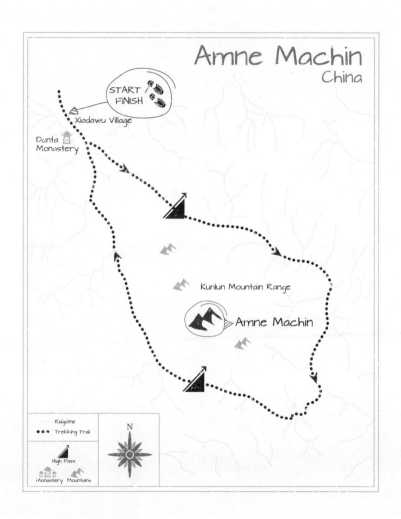

Amne Machin

With an elevation of 6282 m (20,610 ft) ASL, Amne Machin—known to the Chinese as Animaqing Shan—is the highest mountain in a range of the same name and the 23rd highest mountain in China.

The vast Amne Machin mountain range, which emerges from high-altitude grassland that stretches for hundreds of kilometers in every direction, runs roughly northwest to southeast across eastern Qinghai Province. The range is a continuation of the Kunlun Mountains, which extend for more than 3000 km (1864 miles) across Asia from the Tibetan Plateau in western China to the far side of the North China Plain in the east.

The first European to describe Amne Machin was the British soldier and explorer Brigadier-General George Pereira, who set off on an expedition to the region in 1921. Joseph Rock wrote about it too, in his 1930 article for National Geographic, but once again made a mis-calculation and overestimated its height. It wasn't until 1960 that the mountain was first climbed, and it would be another 20 years before its height was accurately surveyed and recorded.

/ 4 \

One of the problems inherent in trekking in the mountains is that every mountain is different. Obviously, it's worth trawling the Internet for suggested routes and other potentially useful information, but it's important to remember that other people's experiences aren't necessarily a very accurate indicator of what your own will be.

When we set out to circumambulate Amne Machin, I was less anxious and uncertain than I had been before our journey to Minya Konka, not least because I had a sense that, this time, I knew what I was doing. Having successfully completed one trek, I felt I had a better understanding of the elements I had to prepare for. Most importantly of all, I knew I didn't have to plan every single aspect down to the last detail: I was pretty sure that, using the experience we'd gained on the first trek, we would be able to figure things out as we went along.

I didn't exactly feel that I was in control—I knew even before the journey to Minya Konka that anyone who chooses to battle with nature is getting themselves involved in what will ultimately be a very uneven fight. But I had confidence in my physical abilities and, having reviewed the film footage we had already taken, I believed we were crafting a worthwhile and educational story.

Following the pilgrims' path around Amne Machin was going to be quite different from the previous trek. This time, instead of ascending and descending through a series of deep valleys and beside glacial rivers, we would be walking for a lot of the time through a relatively flat high-altitude plateau as we encircled the mountain.

On 7th August 2013, Chad and I boarded a plane in Shanghai for the 3½-hour flight to Xining, the capital of Qinghai Province.

Our translator and fixer this time was a middle-aged man named Gonpo, who was local to Qinghai Province and who met us at the airport and took us to our hotel in the city.

A significant proportion of Qinghai is comprised of remote grassland plateau, and although it's the fourth largest province in China, it's the third smallest in terms of its population. Like many other Chinese cities, Xining is currently going through a phase of rapid development and there are many indicators on its streets of burgeoning business activity and personal wealth, including a substantial number of Porsches, BMWs, and other luxury European vehicles.

Life had been fairly hectic during the three weeks since we had completed the trek around Minya Konka, and by the time I arrived in Xining, I was tired and feeling a bit flat, the way you do when you've been really busy and then your adrenalin level drops back to normal. I knew it would rise again though, as soon as we got out into the mountains and started our next 'extreme trek'!

The following morning, we packed up, ate our breakfast at the hotel, and then waited for Gonpo and the driver, who turned up two hours late, at 11.00. When I had spoken to Gonpo on the phone a week earlier, we had agreed that he would organize things locally. But, for some reason, he had left it until that morning to try to find a driver for the eight-hour journey to the village of Xiadawu, where we would start our trek.

In a high-altitude region that's bitterly cold and inhospitable for eight months of the year, you get a lot of tourists in the summertime—mostly Chinese escaping the intense heat in eastern cities like Shanghai and Beijing. With so many tourists in the area, finding a driver could prove problematic even a week in advance. Leaving it until the day we were due to set out was ridiculous, and infuriating. It certainly didn't provide us with the problem-free, efficiently managed start to our journey I had hoped for.

On our previous trek, around Minya Konka, Tersing's calm, easy company, understanding of our requirements, and determination to ensure that we were able to do all the filming we needed to do had made him a positive asset. Amne Machin was on his home territory, so we'd hoped he would be able to come with us again.

> ## Tibetan time
>
> Although, geographically, China spans five time zones, since the start of the Cultural Revolution there has been just one standard time throughout the country, which equates to Coordinated Universal Time (UTC) + 8 hours.
>
> In Tibet and Xinjiang, however, UTC + 6 is often used unofficially—which would put our translator and driver bang on time that morning!

Unfortunately though, he had already been pre-booked by a larger group, so he had recommended Gonpo, who—if the first morning was anything to go by—wasn't going to be the same caliber assistant as Tersing.

The original plan was that after Chad and I had been picked up at the hotel at 09.00, we would drive to a local grocery store to buy everything we were going to need for the next eight days, and then head south to Xiadawu. Part of the deal I had worked out with Gonpo was that we would buy all the food and he would do the cooking, using equipment he provided himself—as the guides normally do. In reality, he hadn't brought anything with him at all, and after we'd been to the grocery store, we had to make another, unscheduled, stop to buy a cooker, propane gas, a wok, and all the other basic gear and utensils he was going to need.

It wasn't a huge deal in the greater scheme of things; just an unnecessary irritation. The real issue was that it's important to feel you can trust a guide who is about to lead you into unknown, possibly hazardous mountain territory. So far, I didn't have the same confidence in Gonpo's judgment or commitment to the job in hand as I'd had with Tersing.

Interestingly, when I look back on it now, it seems that the new Ryan was already beginning to emerge, and instead of losing it, as I might have done in the past, I simply took a deep breath and tried to adjust my mental clock to somewhere between city and Tibetan time.

The grocery store in Xining didn't have much fresh produce. So after we had been driving for about three hours, we stopped in a small village to buy more fruit and vegetables. By the time we were approaching Xiadawu, I was tired and beginning to feel anxious about the confusion and uncertainty that had marred the first day.

My spirits lifted a bit as we turned off the main road—heading off the beaten track onto a dirt road is always exciting. And they rose still further at the sight of the amazing gateway constructed of metal poles adorned by hundreds of prayer flags that marks the entrance to the village and to the Amne Machin region.

When you're walking in the mountains, you ascend slowly, so your body has time to acclimatize. Within a period of about 24 hours, we had traveled from what is in effect sea level in Shanghai, to 2275 m (7464 ft) above sea level in Xining, and then to 3700 m (12,139 ft) ASL in Xiadawu—which is in the very high-altitude zone in terms of altitude sickness. By the time we had lifted all our heavy bags out of the car, I had a pounding headache and was struggling to catch my breath.

In comparison to all the prayer flags flapping in the wind like a vast flock of multicolored birds at the gateway, Xiadawu itself was mundane. Basically just one dusty dirt street lined on both sides by small, drab, single-story brick houses and tin-roofed shacks, the only thing that was stirring in the wind was garbage from the village. There was clearly nothing there to entice our driver to stay and rest after the long drive. It was about 07.00—and still light—when we arrived, and as soon as we had found somewhere to stay, unpacked our bags, and paid him, he turned his car around and set off on another eight-hour journey back to Xining.

There are few, if any, phones in remote villages like Xiadawu, so you can't book a room in a guesthouse in advance. You just have to turn up and look for the one with the cleanest beds. On our trek to Minya Konka, we had stayed at the guesthouse owned by a man called Jangbu and his family, where'd we slept in clean, comfortable bunk beds. This time, we spent the night in a truck-stop guesthouse, where there were no friendly faces or laughing children, and no one to cook us a hot, delicious meal. So, as soon as Chad and I had locked all our bags in our room, we walked with Gongpo down the dirt road and found a Muslim restaurant where we had a very good meal of beef noodles.

I didn't sleep well that night. It had been warm in Xining, but at 3700 m (12,139 ft) it was bitterly cold, even in August. We were much further north than we had been at Minya Konka, which also made a difference to the temperature, and we were on a high plateau, where there was nowhere to hide from the wind. Not only was it significantly colder than I had expected it to be, Xiadawu was noisy too, particularly for somewhere so remote and sparsely populated. As well as the sound of the wind, which roared and ripped through the village all night, I was woken up repeatedly by the incessant howling and barking of every dog for miles around. There are vast numbers of wild and semi-wild dogs throughout Tibet, as well as domestic ones that are kept outside, and there must have been at least ten within a stone's throw of the guesthouse we were staying at. Maybe the wind makes them bark, or maybe it's the cold, or the darkness, or fear, or the presence of other dogs.

It's the same at the start of any journey: it takes time to get used to it all—the food, the environment, the altitude, the weather, and, in this case, the dogs. The first 48 hours are always the most difficult as you adjust to being without all the comforts of the city and begin the process of toughening up again. It's an exciting time too, knowing that you're on the verge of a new adventure.

We had planned a rest day for the next day, to allow time for our bodies to adjust to the altitude. We went back to the Muslim restaurant where we'd eaten the previous evening for a breakfast of noodles, fried eggs, and hot Tibetan bread. Then, while Chad cleaned and prepared our camera equipment, I went back to bed and slept for the rest of the morning. It seemed that the dogs were finally sleeping too, and this time there was no barking to keep me awake.

When I woke up, we had some lunch and Chad and I discussed our plans for the journey that lay ahead, while Gonpo found two local yak herders who were free to come with us. After a brief walk around the village, I went back to bed again and when I woke up before dinner, the intensity of the headache I'd had since the previous day had begun to diminish. We ate at the same Muslim restaurant that evening. Then I fell into a deep sleep that not even wind and barking dogs could disturb.

Gautama Buddha

Gautama Buddha—known in India as Siddhartha Buddha—is the Supreme Buddha on whose thoughts and teachings Buddhism is based.

Gautama Buddha is believed to have been born in eastern India, in what is now Nepal, at some time during the fifth or fourth century BCE. But as no contemporary written records about his life or teachings have ever been found, scholars hesitate to make claims about the historical facts. It is probable, however, that he gained enlightenment at Bodh Gaya, founded a monastic order in India, and taught his followers a Middle Way between sensual indulgence and the pursuance of spiritual goals through strict abstinence from worldly pleasures.

As well as being important to Buddhists, some Hindus believe Gautama Buddha to be an avatar of Vishnu, some Muslims consider him to be a prophet, and to those of the Bahá'í faith he is the manifestation of God.

When I woke up on the morning of day three, feeling well rested and more acclimatized, we went back to the gateway at the entrance to the village and did some filming. Despite the still powerful wind, which seemed to be intent on dragging the flailing prayer flags from their moorings, the sun was shining and the sky was a brilliant blue.

Back in the village, we waited with Gonpo for the arrival of our two guides, four yaks, and the donkey that would carry our camera equipment. It was just a two-hour walk to the Danta Monastery, which was as far as we planned to go that day. When we arrived in mid-afternoon, we pitched our tents on the flat grassland beside it. It was our first taste of what was to become a recurring theme on this journey. Without the ups and downs of the terrain or the protection that had been provided by the high slopes of the valleys of Minya Konka, we were constantly exposed to the sun and the wind, as well as more prone to suffering the effects of altitude sickness.

When we finally managed to anchor our tents safely to the ground, we put our bags inside them and walked across the grass to the monastery. With its golden roofs and vivid murals painted in reds, yellows, blues, greens, and gold on already colorful walls, it was a beautiful building and a haunting space. The monk who let us in didn't seem to know much about the building, which appeared to be quite newly built and almost empty. But he was happy to wait while I stood in front of the magnificent altar flanked on either side by hundreds of tiny statues of Buddha, lit a yak-butter candle and asked Gautama Buddha to keep us safe on our journey around the sacred mountain of Amne Machin.

Because we were already at a high altitude, we could only see the peaks of the mountains around us, many of which are more than 6000 m (19,685 ft) ASL. At the same altitude on Minya Konka, the landscape had been barren and rocky, with very little visible soil. Here, there was grass as far as the eye could see. Although we didn't see many wild animals on our treks, Gonpo assured us that there are a lot of small nocturnal creatures living under the ground in the grasslands. He knew the Tibetan names of the few we saw during the daytime, but they didn't translate directly into English, so I never did find out what they were. Except for one, which was the size of a small dog, bounded across the grass like a hare, and I think was some sort of marmot, similar to the North American groundhog.

When we came out of the monastery, we sat near our campsite and watched the sun move slowly towards the distant horizon, set fire to the sky, then disappear from view, taking with it all the light and warmth of the day. The plummeting temperature and strengthening wind drove us into our tents early that night—and on most other nights during the journey. But it was the mornings that were the worst part of every day.

When I woke up on the morning of day four, my tent was covered—inside and out—by a layer of ice. It took a very determined effort of will to leave the warmth of my sleeping bag and step outside, and it wasn't until we'd packed up the tents and were eating our breakfast that the sun began to rise. Within the space of about 90 minutes, the temperature increased significantly by the time we had finished eating, I'd peeled off several layers of clothing and was warm in just a T-shirt.

After breakfast, as we headed out on our first real day of trekking, we saw an even more spectacular display of prayer flags than

Mani stones

Mani stones are rocks, slabs or pebbles inscribed by Tibetan Buddhists with mantras—particularly Om mani padme hum (from which they derive their name)—and often placed individually or in mounds beside roads and rivers as prayer offerings.

the one at the entrance to the village, which, until then, had been hidden from our view behind the monastery. Stretching for maybe 400 m (1312 ft) on at least ten poles, each of which was higher than a house, there were thousands of flags, snapping and cracking and being tugged at furiously by the wind, and dozens of *mani* stones, piled into cairn-like mounds about 20 m (66 ft) high.

Tibetan nomads have been visiting the region for hundreds of years, and some of the more faded flags that had been strung up behind the monastery must have been there for a very long time. Somehow, seeing them straining at their tethers in testament to a faith strongly linked with the natural world made me excited again, perhaps because it reminded me that I was about to venture into a completely different world.

Beyond the prayer flags, we continued to walk through a wide valley whose gently rolling slopes were the antithesis of the sharp, angular ridges of Minya Konka. In many places, there was just a trickle of water and we were walking on the riverbed itself, on rocks that in just a few months time would be tumbling and tossing in the swollen river. Dotted along the sides of the valley above us were several of the white tents that are home to semi-nomadic Tibetan yak herders who take their yaks up to the plateaus in the summer to feed on the lush grass.

We had met few people on our journey to Minya Konka. On our trek around Amne Machin we encountered numerous pilgrims, the first of which were two women and a man performing prostrations. Murmuring prayers, they took a couple of steps and then lay facedown on the ground, stood up again, took two or three more steps, and repeated the whole process. They had the inner tubes of bicycle tires strapped to their knees and to the lower part of their arms and there were large wooden slabs attached to the gloves they wore on their hands to protect them from injury as they slid forward and stretched out, full length, on the rough ground.

They weren't young people, and what they were doing was inspirational. Even more extraordinary was the fact that they would continue to do it all the way around the mountain, every day for what would probably be a month or more, carrying with them just a tent and some food. I felt privileged to have witnessed the manifestation of their devotion to their faith and, for a moment, optimistic for humanity as a whole. We hadn't seen anyone performing a *kora* with prostrations on Minya Konka—perhaps the much deeper-cut valleys make it almost impossible. We were to see it several times on the more gentle slopes of Amne Machin, and every time it recalibrated my perspective on my own aches and pains.

For young people, doing a *kora*, with or without prostrations, is like a coming-of-age rite that marks the transition from adolescence to adulthood and proves their commitment to the Buddhist faith. For older Tibetans, there are social reasons, too, for following the mountain trail with friends or other family members. We saw many more pilgrims of all ages during our fourth and final trek around Kawa Karpo at the end of October, when the ground was already frozen and the yaks had been brought down from the high pastures and corralled in farms for the winter. In the height of summer, it's only the older pilgrims, who don't have crops to tend or animals to herd, that can afford the time.

From presenting my work at universities, galleries, and conferences in the USA and UK, I've realized that, because of the fundamental beliefs and ideals of Buddhism, people tend to think that Tibetans are a passive, peace-loving race. It's a stereotype and a misconception, which perhaps is only really understood when you visit the most remote areas of the region. The reality is that you have to be tough to survive the conditions that prevail on the Tibetan Plateau.

A lot of what people in the West think they know about Tibetans is derived from what they hear about the Dalai Lama and Buddhist monks. In reality, just as not every Christian loves his neighbor and only a fraction of a percent of Muslims are violent aggressors,

Joseph Rock

Joseph Rock was 10 years old when he left his home in Austria to accompany his father to Egypt and then to travel with him around Europe. In 1905, at the age of 21, Joseph Rock emigrated to the USA.

After living for a couple of years in New York, Rock moved to Hawaii, where, despite having no real academic qualifications, he became the territory's first official botanist.

From 1922, he began to spend most of his time in southwest China, studying the people and the plants. Rock also undertook many expeditions—including one to the sacred mountain of Minya Konka—which he described in the many articles he wrote for National Geographic magazine. Although not the most renowned or prolific botanist of the time, he made a significant contribution to our knowledge of both the indigenous flora and the people of the region.

During his years in China, Rock witnessed many of the battles that were being fought between Chinese Muslims and Tibetans. When the Ngolok Rebellion ended in 1949 and the communist took over, he returned to Hawaii, where he died in 1962.

very few Tibetans are monks. Most are descended from the ruthless tribes that were still fighting each other when Joseph Rock was exploring the region in the 1920s and 1930s. And although it's true to say that Tibetans *are* friendly and hospitable, in the way nomadic people have to be in order to survive, it's also true that, in many cases, you cross them at your peril.

What Buddhism offers Tibetans is the same thing most religions offer their followers: rewards in the next life. If you're poor and your current life is difficult, it's comforting to know that you can store up riches in the next one by performing a *kora* around a sacred mountain.

We walked alongside the pilgrims for half an hour and then left them behind us as we began theour ascent towards our first the high pass. Walking uphill at high altitude is always a muscle-wearying, breath-suppressing chore. But it wasn't otherwise a very difficult ascent, because although the valley became narrower as we got higher, it still retained a relatively gentle slope. At the pass—which, at 4250 m (13,944 ft) above sea level, is only slightly higher than the monastery—we had our first, stunning view of the snowy peaks of the eastern edge of the Amne Machin mountain range and Gonpo gave us little squares of paper with horses and other designs printed on them, which we threw up into the air to be caught by the wind and carried to Buddha.

As the wind continued to sweep across the sky, whipping the prayer flags into a fluttering frenzy, it blew dark clouds in front of the sun and within minutes we were engulfed in a snowstorm. With the intensity of the storm increasing, we headed down into the narrow valley on the other side of the pass. Then the sun came out again and the temperature rose rapidly.

We made our camp that night at a more comfortable altitude of 3400 m (11,155 ft), pitching our tents next to a small stream whose crystal-clear water served as both swimming pool and bath and helped ease the aching weariness in my muscles and joints.

Finding a good camping site can have a very positive effect on your morale, and while I was putting up my tent, I realized I was enjoying our journey to Amne Machin. That evening, I also became aware that some of the extraneous junk I had been storing in my brain was being pushed out and nature was percolating in to fill the void. After a good dinner, I went to bed feeling excited about the journey ahead.

/ 5 \

The prayer flags that festooned the slopes beside the river where we camped on day four made me think again about the pilgrims we met on our journey. I really admired their cheerful, patient dedication, particularly the people who were doing the *kora* with prostrations. I'm a sportsman by nature and by nurture, and I get a lot of satisfaction from rising to meet a challenge. But I cannot imagine any possible scenario—except one that involved saving the lives of my wife and children—that would prompt me to do what they were doing, for even a fraction of the distance. I simply cannot envisage believing in anything that would make me do that. Clearly though, the pilgrims we met on all our treks had an absolute belief that they were earning themselves good karma and absolving their sins so that they would reap rewards in the next life. Even if you can't understand or relate to that sort of religious faith, you have to admire their fortitude.

That night, I was woken up by the sound of something scratching and digging very close to my tent. With my heart racing, I eased open the flap just enough to be able to look outside. Chad had heard it too and as the beam of his torch flashed through the darkness, we saw a wolf looking at us with huge yellow eyes that appeared to be full of evil intent. Without moving any other part of my body, I slid my hand very slowly over the ground, picked up a handful of stones, and started throwing them at the animal. Chad had obviously had the same idea and, in the face of our combined barrage, the creature turned and slunk away into the night.

The next morning, we discovered that Gonpo had left out most of the food we'd been carrying with us—which would have fed all five of us for the remaining three or four days of our journey. The wolf must have smelt it and had eaten all our meat. As well as being expensive, that meat was our only source of the protein that was an essential part of our diet while we were pushing our bodies so hard. Even more annoying than having lost it all was Gonpo's apparent lack of concern when he told me what had happened. It was such a basic mistake, and a good example of how important it is to have a guide who's in tune with what you're trying to do.

If we had been in the city, I would probably have fired him. Obviously, that wasn't an option in the mountains, where our mutual survival depended in many ways on us staying together. There wasn't any point yelling at the guy either: it might have provided me with an outlet for my irritation, but it wasn't actually going to help in any way. So, instead of losing it, I told him I was disappointed and that it had been his responsibility. Then I got on with the day.

It was bitterly cold when we woke up on the morning of day five (day three of walking). There was frost on the ground, a layer of ice on all the tents, and a solid block of ice in a bowl where we had left water the night before. Packing up a stiff, frozen tent isn't something easily accomplished while wearing gloves, and without them your fingers throb and burn. Dismantling the campsite is good for your body though: getting your limbs moving again after a night in a sleeping bag is a great way of starting the process of warming yourself up. And then you really get the blood flowing by eating a bowl of hot oatmeal, muesli, raisins, and honey, and drinking a flask of steaming hot powdered Nescafé. (For someone who's a bit of a coffee connoisseur, that's something I never thought I would hear myself say!)

We set out that day along a twisting, turning path that took us through narrow river valleys and onto verdant, high-plateau grassland. We had only been walking for about half an hour when the sun came out and I was able to swap my warm hat for a sun hat and peel off layers of clothing until I was down to just a T-shirt. Everyone has a different style of walking: Chad often walked with his hands in his pockets, whereas I tend to loop my thumbs through the straps of my backpack. So, when the sun was as hot as it was that morning, I wore white gloves to protect my hands from severe sunburn.

The sun retained its heat quite late into the afternoon and it was still warm when we set up our camp on a flat area of grassland. There were yaks and horses grazing on the slopes around us, and in the distance we could see more nomad white tents. We had stopped at that particular spot simply because it was level and therefore a convenient place to pitch our tents. We weren't in any hurry to get to the end of our journey, so we didn't feel the need to push ourselves the way we'd done on our first trek. Because we were carrying our food with us—what was left of it after the wolf had picked it over—almost anywhere could become a campsite where we could eat, rehydrate, and sleep.

At times in my working life, when I'm attempting to control dozens of projects and keep them all moving forward, I feel as though I'm trying to herd cats or catch eels with my bare hands. I don't generally like to leave anything to chance, so it was interesting to realize that knowing you *can* control things is sometimes more stressful than being at the mercy of the elements. If you have options, you have to make decisions. On the Middle Kingdom and India Rides, my adventure motorcycle productions, those options and decisions involved things like whether to take one road and avoid the worst of the traffic, or another one, which might add another day and more expense to an already very expensive adventure. In the mountains, the psychological process is much simpler: we are going to be traveling a certain distance over a number of days, depending on the weather and on how well we cope with the altitude; we have enough food for the worst-case scenario; so let's go!

You have to be prepared in every practical way for your journey. But, once you're on the mountain, it's liberating to wake up every morning knowing that the only thing you have to do is walk. You're either going to sweat and get sunburned or be so wet and cold you can barely think—or, more likely, all of the above; and then, eventually, you're going to find your stride, both figuratively and literally. When you do, you'll reach an almost Zen-like state in which nothing matters except the beauty of your surroundings and the echo of your own footsteps.

Sometimes, though, even on a relatively undemanding trek, there are decisions that do need to be made, and when that happens, it's useful to have enough facts on which to base them. When we reached the level area of grassland where we camped that day, Gonpo asked us if we wanted to stay there or carry on a bit further. In response to my question about how far it was to the next suitable campsite, he told me, 'You can make a camp anywhere. There are a lot of good sites between here and the next high pass, which is about a day's walk away.' To me, that meant there was no reason to push on. If I'd had more accurate information and had known what really lay ahead, I would have made a different decision.

Chad and I were in good spirits that evening. While we were eating our dinner under a cloudless sky, we had a bet about who could stay out longest once the sun set, the temperature plummeted, and the wind got up. Losing the bet was a small price to pay for being warm in my sleeping by 20.30.

I woke up on day six after a really good night's sleep feeling rested, cheerful, and ready to go. We would be heading up to our second high pass, which meant that it was going to be a tough day, and probably the longest of our journey. With luck, it would also be the day on which we would see Amne Machin, the sacred mountain, for the first time.

After a hasty breakfast, we loaded up the yaks and donkey and set off. We were walking alongside a fast-moving glacial river, which we had to cross repeatedly. The first time it was quite fun. Then the previously gentle valley slopes became steep, the river had cut a twisting path through the narrow gorge, and it became more difficult. Having taken off my boots, socks, and pants, and waded through icy waters a few times, it began to feel as though my muscles were drawing on drastically depleted energy reserves and I struggled to keep my balance.

It was mid-afternoon when we reached the spot where we would cross the river for the last time. As we were approaching it, I had noticed a solitary yak sitting amongst the rocks just above us. I didn't think anything of it: we must have passed hundreds of yaks along the way, even the most curious of which had barely stopped grazing long enough to raise their heads and glance at us. Our own yaks and our guides had crossed the river and I was getting ready to wade in after them when, out of the corner of my eye, I saw something move. I turned my head sharply just as a yak, with its head down like an enraged bull, charged at the donkey carrying our camera equipment. I shouted, but there was nothing anyone could do. No more than a few arms lengths away from where I was standing, the yak smacked into the side of the donkey, lifting it up into the air as if it weighed nothing at all.

Fortunately, it was a female yak, so it didn't have the massive, pointed horns the males have. It was lucky, too, that the donkey landed on its feet and was able to stagger away, bruised, bemused, but otherwise unharmed, while the furious, snorting yak looked around for its next target. As the creature lowered its head again, it was apparent that, this time, it had Gonpo in its sights. When the yak charged, Gonpo just managed to dart out of the way. Then the guides threw rocks and stones that eventually stopped it in its tracks long enough for us to be able to gather up our pack animals and make our escape.

Another fortunate aspect of what might have been a game-changing incident was the fact that no damage had been done to our camera equipment. If it had been strapped to the donkey's sides, rather than secured to the top of its back, it would have received the full impact of the blow from the yak's head. Even so, it was a very unnerving experience that left us all feeling very shaken.

What it also did, however, was go some way towards vindicating my—I hesitate to use the word 'fearful'—reaction on my Minya Konka journey during the salt-feeding episode when I had 'helped' the nomad who'd been kraaling his young yaks for the night. Our guides told us later that yaks tend to stick together, as protection against predators, and that although they *are* generally passive animals, it's a good idea to be wary if you see one on its own, away from the rest of the herd. The solitary yak we encountered that day clearly had some serious psychosocial issues.

While the curious incident of the yak in the day-time was un-folding, my heart was pounding. When something happens to raise your heart rate at that sort of altitude, you start to hyperventilate. And that's scary, because when you're already fighting for breath, you wouldn't be able to run—quite literally—to save your life. So all we could do was *walk* away from the attacking animal, We didn't stop walking until there was a very considerable distance between us. And by the time the adrenalin stopped pumping, I felt drained of energy. But as we still had a long way to go that day, I simply had to get over it and carry on.

Afterwards, we laughed about the yak attack. At the time, it was frightening, and it changed the mentality of the day. We all knew it could have ended very differently, and very badly, both for the donkey and for us.

When we reached the end of the valley, we came out again onto a high plateau, where walking on the grassland wasn't the relatively pleasant, easy experience it had been before. Constantly having to step in and out of the dips and furrows that pockmarked the ground was foot-and-ankle-achingly exhausting. I had started the day feeling optimistic. Some 28 km later, I was engulfed by bleak exhaustion.

The high pass we were heading for is 4280 m (14,042 ft) ASL. As we got close to it, the ground leveled out and became almost flat again. Then we saw all the prayers flags and a pile of rocks in the distinctive shape of a *chorten*. And beyond the prayer flags, high above the green grassland, rose the permanently snow-covered peak of the sacred mountain of Amne Machin, glowing yellow-red in the light cast by the late-afternoon sun.

It was easy to understand why, out of all the mountains that surround it, *this* is the mountain Tibetan Buddhists, as well as fol-lowers of other religions, hold to be sacred. Even to someone like me, who has no religious beliefs, it looked mystical. It's difficult to explain—or understand—the feeling of awe I experienced as I looked at it. All my physical aches and pains suddenly seemed to disappear and I had a very real sense that what I was seeing was important. I felt blessed and hugely privileged to be witnessing one of nature's most spectacular creations, not least because I knew that if the sun hadn't been shining at that moment, we wouldn't have seen it at all.

When I had been planning the treks, I'd known that it was taking a risk to allow just one day at the high passes where—weather permitting—we would be able to see the sacred mountains. If I had been trekking solely for my own amusement, it would have been disappointing to find that the clouds were obscuring the view. When one of the main purposes of my journeys was to produce a television documentary, not seeing one of the mountains, or maybe any of them—which was certainly a possibility—would have been a disaster.

We stayed up on the high pass for about an hour, filming, photographing, and trying to absorb the splendor of the mountain. Then we moved on, anxious to reach a lower, more comfortable altitude where we could set our camp before it got dark. In fact, we ended up ascending slightly from the high pass and camping beside the first stretch of river we came across that had clean water for drinking and cooking. You would think that all the glacial water running off the mountains at that altitude would be pure, but in a lot of places it was full of dirt, rocks, and debris that had been swept up in the tumbling, swirling maelstrom of the river's descent. Even filtered and boiled, water like that isn't very pleasant to drink.

It was getting dark by the time we stopped. From a physical point of view, it had been a truly horrible day; a day when I had seriously wondered if I'd finally had enough. Every single part of my body ached, including, but not limited to, my feet, knees, back, and head. At another time, on another mountain, we could have had freezing rain and snow to contend with. Instead, I was sunburned, wind-burned, and suffering from altitude sickness. We had walked for 26 arduous, back-breaking kilometers (16 miles). It didn't help to know that was a considerably greater distance than we would have had to walk if Gonpo had given me all the facts and we had pushed on a bit further the previous day.

It had been the hardest day we'd had, on this trek or on Minya Konka. By the end of it, my spirits had been trampled on by yaks and then lifted up again by the incredible beauty of Amne Machin.

Chorten

The Tibetan Buddhist chorten developed from the pre-Buddhist burial mounds known as stupas.

Chortens can be constructed to contain holy relics—of Buddha or his disciples—or mantras, as places of meditation, to commemorate visits, and for the purpose of gaining positive karma. Destroying a chorten is considered to be a serious act that will lead to problems of rebirth.

Chortens, stupas, and pagodas can range in size and complexity from simple mounds of earth or rocks—added to by passing pilgrims—to huge gilded edifices made of elaborately carved stone.

Between them, and in different ways, both experiences had drained every last drop of my energy. That evening, when recording my video diary, I was unable to hold back the tears that were the physical manifestation of exhaustion and mixed emotions.

While we were eating a hastily prepared meal, the temperature started to drop and I was glad to be able to seek the shelter of my tent. Just a few hours earlier, I had been looking in awe at the sacred mountain of Amne Machin. As I crawled into my sleeping bag, my spirits were at an all-time low.

Before setting out on our first journey, I had wanted to be faced with challenges that would test my physical endurance and push me to my limits. That night, as I lay in my tent, there was no pleasure or satisfaction to be derived from knowing that I'd got what I had wished for.

There were nights on all the mountain treks when I went to bed feeling gloomy and full of self-doubt. And there were nights when I really thought that, this time, I might have pushed myself too far and would wake up the next morning to find that I didn't bounce back and wasn't able to carry on walking. (There were nights, too, when I even wondered if I might be going mildly insane.) In reality, of course, there wasn't any choice about walking or not walking. When you are thousands of meters above sea level, on the side of a remote mountain where there are no roads, no other people, and no phone or Internet access, there is only one way down.

I'm quite an emotionally stable person, and my 'normal' life in the city involves few emotional ups and downs. Like most people, I do what needs to be done to ensure that everything is organized in such a way as to protect me and my family from all but the smallest of irritations. In the mountains, however, there are times when you don't know how to feel. Surprisingly perhaps, for someone as pragmatic as I am, I quite enjoyed that aspect of the treks. I don't know why. I suppose I had a sense of achievement knowing that I'd had real obstacles to deal with in difficult situations and I had come through. Every time I stayed the course, my confidence increased. And so did my sense that when I went back to the city, I would be able to manage whatever life threw at me—as long as it didn't involve being attacked by a yak.

I slept well that night, sheer exhaustion overriding the discomfort of being at an altitude of 4386 m (14,390 ft), which was the highest we had set our camp on the journey so far.

When I woke up the next morning, a quick check of the thermometer confirmed my impression that it was well below freezing inside my tent. A cautious examination of my spirits indicated that they had bounced back from the low of the previous night, and when I stepped outside, they soared. To the east, the sun was rising over Amne Machin; to the west, it was beginning to cast its golden light on the slopes of the grassland valley that stretched far into the distance, illuminating the nomads' tents and the many peacefully grazing yaks.

We tend to take for granted whatever's familiar to us, and as I looked at that incredible landscape, I wondered if the nomadic herders are so used to it they barely notice it. Or do they step out of their tents every morning and feel their spirits soar because they know they're living in one of the most beautiful places on Earth?

The light that morning was clear and sharp. Normally, I would have reached for my camera, or woken Chad so that he could capture the moment on film. Instead, I just stood there, mesmerized by the beauty that surrounded me and with a strange sense that I was the only person in the entire world who was witnessing the sun rise above the sacred mountain of Amne Machin.

We had another hard walk ahead of us that day, so as soon as

Trekkers' feet

When you walk day after day in the mountains, your feet take an absolute beating. The fact that you're walking for most of the time on uneven ground means they're constantly rubbing against the inside of your boots. Inevitably, you get a lot of blisters, particularly on the bottom of your feet at the base of your toes, on the toes themselves, on your heels where they come into contact with your boots . . . The skin around the base of your heels is prone to cracking and bleeding too. And if you sweat—which you will do, either because the ambient temperature is high or from exertion when it's low—your socks and the inside of your boots will be permanently wet, as a result of which you'll develop rashes on your feet as well.

Basically, your feet are sore all the time. But when you get going in the mornings, you just push the discomfort into the background and try to forget about it. When you've got a lot of ground to cover in just a few hours, there are plenty of other, more pressing, matters to occupy your mind. In any case, there's really nothing you can do about your feet until you've finished walking for the day.

On the days when we set our camp early, when the sun was still strong, I'd take off my boots and socks, pop as many blisters as I could, put antiseptic on the raw, exposed skin, and then let the sunlight dry them out. Within a couple of days, the old damaged skin would have peeled off and the layer beneath it would be slightly less tender.

When you're walking in the mountains, blisters are simply an occupational hazard. (And if you want to be taken seriously as an explorer or adventurer, you don't want anyone to hear you bitching about your feet!)

Disclaimer. I looked it up, and apparently my way of dealing with blisters isn't the approved way. You're not supposed to pop them. You're supposed to make sure the skin remains intact to avoid infection; cover them with soft dressings, which should be changed daily; always wash your hands before you touch them; and (I quote) '. . . if the blister is on your foot, avoid wearing the shoes that caused it, at least until it heals.' My way worked for me, but I just want to make it clear that I'm not advocating it—for legal reasons!

we'd packed up our tents and eaten our breakfast, we got back on the trail. Despite making slow progress through the endless grasslands, over uneven, water-logged ground, I felt that nothing could dampen my spirits. Nature seemed to be doing her best though, as if to reestablish her authority after her generosity the previous day. The sun shone, hot and relentless, in a sky devoid of clouds, and the wind ripped across the plateau as if hell-bent on sweeping away everything in its path. There were no deep river valleys to shelter us from the wind, and no mountain peaks to cast their shadows and protect us from the sun, as there often had been on our trek around Minya Konka. There were only gentle slopes and sky that rose above an infinite horizon like an immense blue dome. Except for one brief interlude when we ascended to cross a river and then climbed up out of the valley onto the flat grassland again, we were exposed to the elements for the entire day.

That morning, I stood outside my tent looking at Amne Machin with tears in my eyes, believing that nothing could ever dampen my spirits again. By the afternoon, we had walked nearly as far as the previous day and I was sunburned, exhausted, and longing for the day to end.

When we reached the road that marked the end of our journey to the sacred mountain of Amne Machin we had walked an eternity. The following day, a car would come to take us back to civilization. I felt an enormous sense of relief knowing that we had done what we had set out to do. But I felt sad, too. Every trek raised questions in my mind. Would I ever see the mountain again? Was what I was doing giving me a new lease of life or slowly killing me? Was I learning things about myself, or simply pushing my body repeatedly to the point of collapse for no good reason? The end of a long, wearying journey wasn't the time to try to find the answers.

We set our camp near the road and had just eaten our dinner and settled into our tents when it started to hail. I had come a long way, in many respects, from the first night of the first trek when the sound of rain falling on my tent had kept me awake. On this night, the thunder of hailstones was strangely soothing, and my last thought before I fell asleep was that I was proud of what we had accomplished.

I stepped out of my tent the next morning as three red-robed monks walked past our campsite. As I watched them striding along the road in the morning sunshine, I was struck by the thought that, in some indefinable but positive way, we were connected. It was a realization that made me smile.

We didn't know how long we would have to wait before our driver picked us up, or how much further along the road we would have to walk to find him. We had told him roughly when and where to meet us, but without a mobile phone, there was no way of letting him know we'd arrived.

It would have been reasonable to assume that we had already exhausted our combined stock of good karma. But we had just eaten our breakfast and packed up all our bags when a car rounded a bend in the road. Within minutes, we were on our way back to Xiadawu village, where, eight days earlier, our incredible journey had begun.

The best months to travel to Amne Machin are September and
October.

The average altitude of the land surrounding Amne Machin is
approximately 3500–4000 m (11,500–13,000 ft). Its physical
features of high grassland, glacial lakes, and deep canyons define
this part of southern Qinghai Province. In winter, the area is covered by snow and there are strong winds. In summer, the heat can
be suffocating and the risk of altitude sickness is compounded by
sun damage and dehydration.

The trek begins and ends in the unremarkable town of Xiadawu
(3700 m / 12,139 ft) in Jiangxi Province, where you should be able
to source guides with yaks to accompany you on your expedition.

Be sure to spend a night or two in Xiadawu to acclimatize to the
altitude before continuing south into the grasslands.

It will take 7–9 day to complete the trek. Back in Xiadawu, you can
hire a car and driver for the 8-hour drive to Xining, the capital of
Qinghai Province. From Xining, you can take a taxi or bus about
30 km east to Xining Caojiabao Airport. It is currently (January
2015) not possible to fly from Xiadawu to Xining.

How to Get to Amne Machin

Fly to Xining Caojiabao Airport in Qinghai Province, China.

Hire a driver and car for the 8-hour drive south to Xiadawu, where
the driver should be able to direct you to one of the town's many
guesthouses.

In Xiadawu you will also be able to hire guides with yaks and donkeys to accompany you on your trek.

Be sure to stock up on food in the local market Xiadawu.

It's a good idea to stay in Xiadawu for at least a couple of days while
you begin the process of acclimatizing to the altitude before
setting out on your trek.

Potential Costs

The following costs are based on the assumption that you are
traveling alone, rather than in a tour group, and were correct in
October 2013, when US $ 1 = 6.15 Yuan.

Cost of hiring a car and driver from Xining to Xiadawu: 2800 Yuan

Cost per yak/donkey: 200 Yuan per day

Cost per yak handler/guide/cook: 150 Yuan per day

Cost of food: budget for 200 Yuan per person per day

Cost of hiring a car and driver from Xiadawu to Xining Caojiabao
Airport: 2800 Yuan
Note. Costs might fluctuate during high season. Expect to pay more
with a tour group.

How I Completed this Trek
I flew from Shanghai to Xining, where I hired a car and driver for
the journey to Xiadawu.
In Xiadawu, I hired 1 cook and 2 guides with 4 yaks and 3 donkeys.
At the end of the trek, I hired a driver and van for the drive from
Xiadawu back to Xining.
Then I flew from Xining Caojiabao Airport to Shanghai.

Important note. You should be sure to consult a physician before
attempting any high-altitude trekking. Many pilgrims and travelers
to these regions die each year because of health problems and lack
of preparedness. The risks are REAL.

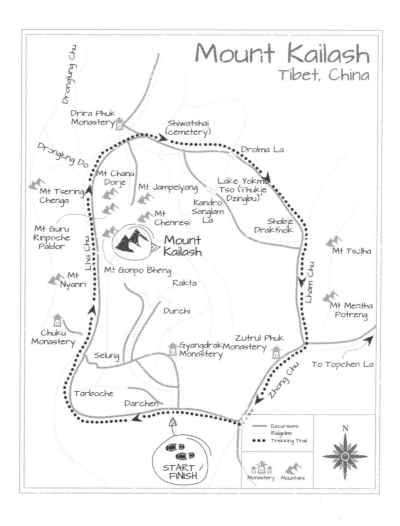

Mount Kailash
Tibet, China

Drongkung Chu

Drira Phuk Monastery

Shiwatshai (cemetery)

Drolma La

Drongkung Do

Mt Chana Dorje

Mt Jampelyang

Lake Yokmo Tso (Thukje Dzingbu)

Mt Tsering Chenga

Kandro Sanglam La

Mt Chenresi

Shabje Drakthok

Mt Guru Rinpoche Paldor

Lha Chu

Mount Kailash

Mt Tsolha

Mt Gonpo Bheng

Rakta

Lham Chu

Mt Nyanri

Durchi

Mt Mentha Potreng

Chuku Monastery

Zutrul Phuk Monastery

Selung

Gyangdrak Monastery

To Topchen La

Tarboche

Darchen

Zhong Chu

START / FINISH

Excursions
Ridgeline
••• Trekking Trail

N

Monastery   Mountains

Mount Kailash

Mount Kailash is part of the Kailas range of mountains in the Trans-Himalayas, the western continuation of the Himalayas in southern Tibet. The glaciers on Mount Kailash and the surrounding mountains are the source of the longest rivers in Asia—including the Indus, Brahmaputra, Karnali (a tributary of the River Ganges) and Sutlej. Mount Kailash has an elevation of 6638 m (21,778 ft) ASL.

Mount Kailash is considered a holy mountain to almost 20% of all the people in the world. Those of Hindu faith believe that the god Shiva resides at its summit. The Bonpo believe that the founder of their religion landed there when he descended from the sky. For Jainists, it is the site where the founder of their religion experienced spiritual awakening. And for Tibetan Buddhists—who call it Rinpoche (meaning 'precious jewel')—it is the home of Buddha Demchok.

Almost 1000 years ago, the Tibetan poet and yogi Jetsun Milarepa wrote about Mount Kailash, 'There is no place more powerful for practice, more blessed, or more marvelous than this. May all pilgrims and practitioners be welcome.' In fact, every year, thousands of pilgrims, including many from India, Pakistan, and Nepal, perform koras on the 52-km (32-mile) trail around the mountain.

Despite some myths and stories, there have been no recorded attempts to climb Mount Kailash. The mountaineer and explorer Reinhold Messner declined the opportunity when it was offered to him by the Chinese government in the 1980s. The offer was made again in 2001, this time to a team of Spanish climbers, but was then withdrawn in the face of international disapproval. It is now forbidden by law to attempt to climb to the summit of Mount Kailash.

/ 6 \

Two days after completing our journey to Amne Machin, I flew home to Shanghai. Less than three weeks later, on 5 September 2013, I left again, this time bound for Lhasa, the capital of Tibet Autonomous Region and, at 3650 m (11,975 ft) above sea level, one of the highest cities in the world. I had been in New York two days earlier and had spent just one day with my family. So I arrived in Lhasa feeling tired and jet-lagged. Within a few minutes of landing at the airport, I was also beginning to suffer the effects of altitude sickness.

We were met on our arrival in Lhasa by our translator and 'fixer', Dorgee. Before we set out on our trek, we were going to spend a couple of days in the city, resting and acclimatizing to the altitude. And as Lhasa had been Dorgee's home since he had moved there from Sichuan Province to work as a guide when he was young man, he had agreed to show us round.

The next day, in an effort to remain active to aid the process of acclimatization, we visited the Jokhang Monastery, which stands in a square amongst the narrow laneways of the old part of the city known as Barkhor. The monastery was built during the seventh century by a Tibetan king for his two wives—one Chinese, the other from Nepal—and it has strong architectural influences from all three countries. The monastery (Jokhang means 'House of Buddha') has had a checkered history. Briefly boarded up by a Bon king in the ninth century, it was subsequently ransacked many times by the Mongols and, more recently, in 1966, by Red Guards during 'the Great Proletarian Cultural Revolution.' The multiple raids destroyed thousands of original Buddhists scriptures in what is the most sacred of all the Buddhist monasteries in the country.

> ## Potala Palace
>
> Before he fled to India during the Tibetan Uprising in 1959, the Potala Palace was the main residence of the Dalai Lama.
>
> Built on rocks on the side of a mountain, it has two distinct and very beautiful buildings: the original white building, where visitors used to go to discuss political matters, and a red building, of later construction, where the monks prayed.
>
> Despite being well cared for and preserved, the palace today has the rather forlorn air of a museum that exists to remind people of something that used to be.

By the time I arrived, there were already hundreds of pilgrims walking around the monastery in a clockwise direction as they performed a *kora*. The early-morning mist was augmented by smoke from incense that was burning in cauldrons near the monastery walls. And the murmuring of many voices was accompanied by the click-clack of prayer wheels and the intermittent clang of a bell.

Before going inside the Jokhang, I did another *kora* at a smaller monastery nearby. And by the time I went up onto its roof, the mist had cleared to reveal an incredible view of the city.

In the afternoon, we went to the Sera Monastery just outside the city. I had been there three years earlier with my brother during 'The Middle Kingdom Ride'—and to the Potala Palace, which we didn't visit again this time. The Sera Monastery is actually a complex comprising numerous hermitages, nunneries, and colleges, which used to house up to 6000 Buddhist monks (now only about 550), and is well known for its 'monk debates.' There were many more tourists that afternoon than there had been during my previous visit. But despite the crowds, it was a good day. Chad shot some great film footage and I had a chance to clear my head of other Shanghai-related work issues and immerse myself in the here and now.

Despite going to bed that night in a positive, upbeat mood, I woke up on day two still feeling jet-lagged and pretty rough. We had a lot of visits planned for the day, as well as some relatively low-intensity trekking. Our first stop was the Drepung monastery.

Located at the foot of Mount Gephel about 5 km outside Lhasa, Drepung is the largest monastery in Tibet. It currently houses about 300 Buddhist monks, but in the 1930s, when it was home to up to 10,000, it was thought to be the largest monastery in the world.

We had no plans to go inside it. Instead, we trekked around it, following a path that led up and down some steep inclines. The *kora* took us about 90 minutes and was exactly what we needed to get our leg muscles working again and allow our lungs to become adapted to breathing the thin air.

The sun was still shining in a clear blue sky when we left the Drepung Monastery and headed back into Lhasa. Our next stop was a market, where I bought some prayer wheels and other tourist trinkets, including a small copper, four-faced Buddha head depicting Buddha laughing, smiling, angry, and sad. I always enjoy the market experience and it was fun to practice my Chinese while bargaining with vendors.

At lunchtime, we went to a small Tibetan noodle shop. After we'd had our meal, the owner let us visit the kitchen to watch the

Monk debates

The four monk debates that take place every day in the 'debating courtyard' of Sera Monastery have become very popular with tourists. However, their primary purpose is educational, to give monks who are studying at the monastery's colleges a better understanding of Buddhist philosophy.

The strict rules and procedures that govern the debates are based on Hindu traditions that were adopted in Tibet from India during the eighth century.

Once a subject has been chosen for a debate, the questioner presents his case, which is always on a Buddhism-related subject. He will then pose questions to the defender, many of which are intended to trick or deceive him. The defender must respond within a set time frame and prove his point of view.

Punctuated by dramatic gestures, hand clapping, shouting, and attempts to unnerve the defender when he gives a wrong answer, the debates are noisy, robust, fantastically visual and entertaining.

cook making the same sort of thick, dry, bland noodles we had just eaten—which are transformed into something really tasty by the addition of spices and vegetables. It was a place Dorgee recommended and there wasn't a single tourist in sight, just some men sitting outside playing a game that involved a cup, dice, and some boisterous laying of bets.

In the afternoon, we asked Dorgee to take us to a shopping mall in town to buy the supplies for our trek. The place we ended up was a new, very high-end mall in the center of town where every shop apart from the grocery store sold faux luxury brands, jewelry, and fancy goods. In modern China, wealthy people are no longer reticent about displaying the trappings of their wealth.

We spent an hour in the grocery store, buying toilet paper, noodles, powdered coffee, peanuts, dried fruit, oats . . . anything that was easy for the pack animals to carry and didn't need to be refrigerated. Then we took it all back to the hotel and repacked it, ready for our flight the following day to Ali, which the largest town in western Tibet and close to the Indian border.

When I woke up at 05.00 on day three in the hotel in Lhasa, it was dark, cold, and raining more heavily than I had ever seen in the city before. It was too early to get any breakfast, so we loaded our bags into the car and headed for the airport.

I had waited 12 years to see Mount Kailash and I could feel my excitement mounting as we boarded the plane. I wanted to visit the mountain when I went to Kashgar on my first trip to China in 2001, but the G219 Highway, which runs from Kashgar to Ali, had just been closed due to the bombings in Afghanistan. In 2010, I'd got close to it again on 'The Middle Kingdom Ride.' I didn't make it that time because Colin and I had been on the road too long to cope with another physical challenge.

There were only about 20 people on board the large Boeing plane that flew us from Lhasa to Ali, so everyone had a window seat and a good view. Almost every mountain we flew over was high enough to have at least a light covering of snow. And then there below us, at last, was Mount Kailash. Instantly recognizable by its distinctive pyramid shape, it was even more spectacular than it looked in any photograph I had ever seen.

When the airport at Ali (known as Ngari Gungsa) opened to civil aviation just four years ago, it became the fourth highest airport in the world, at 4274 m (14,022 ft) ASL. It's probably the fourth coldest too. The air was so dry and thin that the simple act of lifting the bags off the baggage carousel left me winded and fighting for breath.

From the airport, we drove a few hours south to the small village of Darchen, which is the starting point for pilgrimage s to Mount Kailash and nearby Lake Manasarovar, as well as where the necessary permits are issued. We arrived in time to have lunch at the Oceans Family Restaurant, which, despite its name, is some considerable distance from the nearest ocean.

Interestingly, the menu at the restaurant was available in Russian, a sign of changing times and of the fact that vast numbers of Russian tourists are currently visiting Tibet. Keen for a challenge, and perhaps to emulate the macho example of their president, Vladimir Putin, Russians are climbing the highest peaks and trekking the most rugged trails. It's all about being seen to be tough, and—I say this with the greatest of respect—they are quite insane!

While we ate at the restaurant, Dorgee went to the police office to get our permits and papers stamped. Then we drove southwest for another hour towards the border between Tibet and Nepal.

We stayed that night at the Loving Family Guesthouse, a drab, unattractive building close to Lake Manasarovar. Most of the other guests were Tibetan, but later in the evening, while we were eating our dinner, five Russians walked into the dining room. They were probably all in their forties, quite wealthy—judging from their iPhones and expensive watches—and clearly quite pumped, with good reason, as it turned out. Their guide explained to us, via Dorgee, that the five men had just completed a trek around Mount Kailash—a distance of 52 km over some incredibly challenging terrain—in just a day and a half. Apparently, they had set out the previous day and done the normal distance; then they had started walking again the following morning at 03.00 and finished at 15.00. It was a very impressive achievement, which the five men toasted repeatedly throughout the evening as they downed an equally im-

Tibetan high-altitude gene

Most races of people who live and work at altitudes above 4000 m (about 13,000 ft) have more than the normal amount of the oxygen-carrying protein hemoglobin in their blood.

Tibetans are a unique exception to that rule. Their red blood cells actually contain less hemoglobin than normal, possibly as an adaption to avoid the clots and strokes that are associated with thicker blood.

A recent study has identified a 'superathelete' variant of a gene called EPAS1, which is unique to Tibetans and which regulates the production of hemoglobin.

The EPAS1 gene was inherited from an ancient species of humans known as Denisovans, who inhabited Siberia and other parts of Asia and became extinct some 40,000 years ago.

Whereas Han Chinese and other races lost this gene over the years, it was retained, by the process of natural selection, by Tibetans living on the high-altitude Tibetan Plateau.

pressive quantity of Russian vodka. President Putin would have been proud of them.

For the Russians, a swift, tough trek around Mount Kailash was probably a once-in-a-lifetime experience. For the Tibetan guides, it was simply part of everyday life. Dorgee had done it more than 100 times—on the first occasion when he was just 12 years old. Like all the other Tibetan guides, his level of fitness was on completely separate scale. I had often wondered how the guides function with apparent ease at such high altitudes. So I was interested to read recently that Tibetans have a special high-altitude gene.

I slept well that night, despite being woken up several times by the increasingly noisy and emotional celebrations of the Russians. When I heard them leaving for the airport at 05.00, it was hailing, and when I woke up on the morning of day four there was snow on the ground.

A quick dash through wet snow to the outside pit toilet soon chased away any last remnants of drowsiness. By the time we had eaten our breakfast, the snow had stopped falling and the sun was out. We had some acclimatizing to do, which wasn't going to be achieved by sitting around in the guesthouse. It was time to get moving.

We walked up a hill above the clear, sky-reflecting waters of the glacial lake. At the top, there was an old man spinning a prayer wheel and intoning as he performed a *kora* around *mani* stones of every imaginable size, shape, and color.

There were originally eight monasteries around the lake, several of which were destroyed in the Chinese invasion of Tibet. We visited the Chiu Monastery on the western shore, which has been rebuilt into the rocks on the side of a cliff and is the most beautiful monastery I've ever seen in any country. The original building was constructed around a cave where Guru Rinpoche—who introduced Buddhism to Tibet in the ninth century—is once purported to have stayed for a week. There didn't seem to be anyone living in the monastery apart from one very ancient-looking monk who took us to the cave to show us the Guru's footprint embedded in the rock.

We had left the Chiu Monastery and were making our way down to the lake when the sun came out. If I was going to take a dip in its glacial waters, this seemed like the moment to do it.

We arrived at the lake just as a large group of Indian Hindus were leaving it. It would have been good to have shared their experience. But I did get the chance to talk to some of them, including a man called Shiva. Shiva's family was originally from Mumbai, but Shiva was born in the USA and now works in Singapore. He spoke very movingly about what the lake means to Hindus in general and what the pilgrimage he was making meant personally to him.

When the pilgrims moved on, they took with them my last excuse for procrastinating. Taking off my clothes, I waded out into the icy water and dipped under the surface three times, in the Hindu way.

If it's possible for your sins to be *frozen* out of you, the place to do it is Lake Manasarovar. Even before I reached a depth at which ducking under the water became feasible, it felt as though my whole body was on fire. In fact, though, despite the intensity of the cold, it was a strangely invigorating experience. So much so that after I came out of the lake and dried off, I went back in again with a 74-year-old Indian pilgrim from Washington, DC.

There was no heating or indoor plumbing at the Loving Family Guesthouse. Fortunately, there are some hot springs beside the lake. And that's where I headed immediately after my 'double-dip' experience, to try to get some feeling back into my extremities.

If you're used to Western health clubs and spa facilities, the hot springs of Lake Manasarovar might not be quite what you would imagine. In that part of the world, they're more of a bathing necessity for local people than a luxury, and the healthy option might actually be to give them a miss. I paid my money and was given a bit of plastic with which to line the dirty wooden tub before I sat in it. But I was cold and there wasn't a hot shower for miles around. So I shut my mind to the health-and-safety aspects and, for the next 30 minutes, focused instead on the revitalizing, almost-too-warm, water.

Warm again and with sensation restored to my fingers and toes, we went back to the guesthouse. After we had drunk some tea and eaten our dinner, I went to bed feeling pretty positive about what I'd seen and experienced that day.

On the morning of day five, I awoke again to another heavy snowstorm. Although it was very cold in the room at the Loving Family Guesthouse, at least it *was* a room. What was it going to be like being in a tent in that kind of weather? I wasn't going to have to wait long to find out.

After breakfast, we packed up our rooms drove from the relative protection of the sunken lake area to the more exposed grasslands adjacent to Mount Kailash. The plan was to spend a couple of nights in the tents, acclimatizing to the altitude and low temperature, before starting our trek in earnest—and moving on to higher altitudes, lower temperatures, and extreme wind.

The campsite we chose was within sight of Mount Kailash—or would be when the clouds lifted. There were some semi-nomadic yak herders camped nearby and while I was pitching my tent, one of their dogs ran towards me, snarling and barking ferociously. Every instinct was telling me to turn and run. But even before I heard Dorgee's shouted warning, I knew that the dog would run faster. My only real chance of avoiding an attack that might put me in hospital and end our trek before it had even started was by standing my ground.

Without taking my eyes off the dog, I bent down, scooped up as many rocks as I could hold, and started shouting. The dog hesitated for a moment, took a few more steps towards me, and then stood perfectly still, sniffing the air. Was it having second thoughts about attacking me? Or were its hind legs flexing slightly as it prepared to hurl itself at me?

My heart was thudding against my ribs as we both stood there, man and beast, weighing up the situation and deciding what to do next. The beast was the first to make a move. Turning slowly, the dog slunk away in the direction it had come. After a few seconds, I continued with the task of putting up my tent. But I kept a wary eye open, in case the dog was sly and had only pretended to run away so that it could wait until my back was turned and catch me unawares.

The ground was dusty and the air was extremely cold on the grassland. My encounter with the dog had got the blood pumping in my veins and had done a lot to warm me up. Then the clouds suddenly cleared and Mount Kailash appeared like a vast, curved pyramid towering above everything around it.

The down side of the sun coming out was that it raised the air temperature just enough to wake up thousands of mosquitoes, which swarmed around our camp. It was an annoying, although fortunately short-lived, attack and when the clouds blocked the sun again an hour later, the mosquitoes disappeared too.

We started eating quite late that evening, just as the sun was going down. Within minutes, the temperature plummeted and the wind intensified, tearing across the grassland as it chased away the last remnants of the day. Although our meal of yak meat, fried rice, and green peppers was good, I was soon too cold to care about food. So I headed for my tent and the relative warmth of my sleeping bag.

In terms of starting the process of acclimatizing, it had been a successful day. Less reassuring as I fell asleep that night was the thought that our trek hadn't even started and already I was finding the cold was difficult to deal with.

/ 7 \

It was the morning of day six since I had flown from Shanghai to Lhasa, and the day when we would begin our trek to Mount Kailash. The temperature inside my tent was well below freezing. That meant it was probably very cold, windy and bitter outside. My body ached, my joints were stiff, and I had an almost overpowering desire to close my eyes again and go back to sleep. But getting moving was the only way to melt the ice crystals in my veins and get the blood pumping. Telling myself that through discomfort comes enlightenment, I unzipped my sleeping bag and got up.

My effort was rewarded on stepping out of my tent by the sight of an incredible landscape. The grasslands were covered in a layer of frost and Mount Kailash stood out in the morning light like the manifestation of something that had been created in an artist's imagination.

By the time I had packed up my tent, my blood was beginning to flow again. Our nomadic neighbors were packing up that morning too, loading their belongings onto the back of a hug pick-up truck, so I went over to talk to them. They had been in the same spot all summer, they told me, but now it was getting too cold and it was time to move to lower ground.

If it was too cold for semi-nomadic Tibetan herders who were used to tough conditions, was this a good time for us to be setting out on a trek that would take us even higher into the mountains? I knew it was late in the season to be embarking on a *kora* to Mount Kailash. The expressions on the faces of the departing nomads when I told them what we were planning to do made me wonder if it was actually *too* late.

Rather than eat our breakfast out in the open, we packed up and drove to Darchen. It's amazing how quickly hot coffee and banana pancakes can restore your optimism. After breakfast, we picked up our permits and then loaded all our gear onto the bus that would take us to the starting point of our trek, where we would meet up with our guides.

We passed a lot of Indian and Tibetan pilgrims walking along the dusty road en route to the gateway that marks the start of the trail that encircles Mount Kailash. There were even more pilgrims, tourists, and wild dogs milling around where the bus dropped us off. Amongst them were our two guides, with a donkey and three yaks.

Disconcertingly, one of the guides was bleeding heavily from a large cut over his right eye. It turned out that, in his haste to arrive on time to meet the bus, he had pushed his donkey to go faster and had fallen off when the animal slipped. I was sorry for the guy, but impressed and encouraged by his obvious commitment to our venture. Fortunately, there was a first-aid kit in one of our bags, and when we finally managed to stop the bleeding, I cleaned the cut and patched him up. Although he was badly shaken, he insisted that he was fit for the tough journey that lay ahead for us all.

The sun was shining as we walked through hundreds of prayer flags on the other side of the gateway. And as I took the first few steps along the trail and looked up at the south face of Mount Kailash, I felt a rush of excitement.

We could see the same view of the mountain throughout that first day, and for a lot of the time we were in sight of other people, too. Most of the Tibetan pilgrims stopped to chat and exchange high-fives. After having very little contact with people during the previous two treks, the interactions were fun and it was interesting to get a sense of the pilgrimages from a social perspective.

We camped that night at 4800 m (15,748 ft), now with a view of the southwestern face of the mountain. Most of the pilgrims stay at the little teahouses that are dotted along the trail. But I wanted a more 'authentic' experience, so we had walked on a bit further. It seemed like a good decision, until the sun started to go down, the temperature dropped, and the wind grew so strong we had to stack anything we could find around the cooker just to be able to light it.

When you're not eating lunch and you need *something* to look forward to at the end of the day, dinner has to be good. Dorgee did all the cooking—as professionally as he did everything else—and he made a great meal that night, of pasta, green peppers, tomato sauce, and yak meat. By 19.00, it was too cold to be outside. I went to bed with excellent food in my stomach and positive thoughts in my head.

It was 11.00 the next morning by the time the wind speed had dropped from cyclonic to gale force and it was warm enough—just—for being outside to be bearable. There were moments when I wondered if staying in the little teahouses along the way might have been a more sensible option. At least I would have set off every day feeling warm. But I was doing the treks mainly because I wanted to immerse myself in the natural world, not for the religious reasons of the pilgrims. And sleeping on a mat on the floor of a teahouse alongside dozens of other people didn't really fit the brief.

We started walking at about noon that day, as we did every day throughout the trek. Every night followed a pattern, too. I would go into my tent at about 19.00, write in my diary, fall asleep at about 20.00, wake up at 22.30, drink some hot water, go back to sleep until 01.00, wake up and drink some more water, force myself to go outside to get rid of some of the water I'd drunk, crawl back into my sleeping bag wondering if I would ever be warm again, wake up at around 04.00 feeling cold, dehydrated, and suffering from the effects of the altitude. For the next few hours, I would alternate between dozing and lying awake staring at the roof of the tent, willing the sun to rise.

On the second day, we came across some of the 'garbage girls' who walk along the trail picking up discarded candy wrappers and glass bottles. Despite the presence of big blue bins at regular intervals, a lot of the people who gaze in awe at the breathtakingly beautiful, unspoiled landscape as they encircle Mount Kailash dispose of their garbage by dropping it on the ground.

The 'garbage girls' are brilliant and it's thanks to them that the mountainside is actually quite clean. The girls carry maybe 20 bags with them and as they fill each one, they tie off its neck and leave it at the side of the trail to be picked up by the park manager in his truck. They stay overnight at the teahouses and, like Sisyphus condemned for eternity to roll a boulder up a hill, perform a never-ending task.

Among the many people performing the *kora* were two brothers in their early thirties who set off at 03.00 on what was our second morning to do the entire trek in one day, carrying just some food and water in a plastic bag. At the other end of the spectrum were several people we saw turning round and heading back the way they'd come. Although we were at a high altitude—approximately 5000 m (16,404 ft) on the second day—the ground was more or less flat and there were no difficult inclines and declines to negotiate. Clearly though, some people were already finding it too high, too cold, and too grueling to want to continue. We dealt with those problems by taking it easy and not walking for very long on day two.

Despite its harshness, the barren, rocky landscape had a majestic beauty that was in complete contrast to the green grasslands of Amne Machin. After we had been walking for a while on day two, our view of Mount Kailash was blocked by other mountains. We walked for just two hours that day. When we stopped at 16.00, I was already exhausted. The simple act of bending down and standing up again at that altitude left me struggling to fill my lungs with air, and it took us an hour to put the tents up. Then Chad and I did some filming.

Fortunately, as well as being emotionally invested in filming the documentary, Chad is very fit. I don't imagine there are many people who, having trekked for a couple of hours at that altitude, could then dig deep into their reserves of energy and take the footage he took that day. He's a good man to have on your team. What made it even more impressive was the fact that his breathing was labored and he was developing a hacking cough.

I didn't get much sleep that night. I was concerned about whether Chad would make it up to the high pass we would be heading for during the next couple of days. And when I wasn't worrying about that, I was being kept awake by the sound of the wind and the swirling, icy snow.

The next morning, we woke up to our worst-case scenario—a total white-out. The mountains were invisible behind dense clouds and the ground was covered in snow. The prospect of stepping out into what looked like a scene from an apocalyptic movie was daunting. But it was exciting too. This was what I had signed up for. *This was the world created by nature, a world of spectacular landscapes that only she can choose to reveal or conceal.* I understood then why some people had abandoned the trek the previous day. I was born and raised in Canada, so I'm used to snow and mountains. If you've lived your entire life in Mumbai, for example, where the average minimum winter temperature is 20.5°C (68.9°F), you probably couldn't even imagine being somewhere where it's very windy and -20°C (-6°F) every morning.

The eggs Dorgee cooked for our breakfast that morning had gone cold before he transferred them from pan to plate. And when I poured boiling water onto my oatmeal, it immediately froze. The temperature was well below -20°C (-6°F), the wind chill factor made it even colder, and, like the food, our bodies were unable to retain any heat. Nothing grows at that altitude, so there was no wood to make a fire to huddle round. Trying not to think about fires, I stood eating my rock-hard, frozen breakfast while the wind drove needle-sharp snow into my face. The buzz I'd derived from feeling that I was 'communing with nature' was quickly diminishing; in its place, a voice in my head repeated, plaintively, 'I just want to be warm.'

On a morning like that, you almost look forward to battling the wind as you pack up the camp—anything to get your body moving again. The prospect of walking in a snowstorm, possibly through snow that was already deep on the ground, was more intimidating, particularly as we were going to be ascending almost vertically from 5080 m (16,667 ft) to 5630 m (18,471 ft) at the Dromla Pass. Most worrying of all was the fact that Chad's cough was no better and it was clear that he was feeling quite ill. There were only two choices available to us: turn round and go back the way we had come or continue up to the high pass. Chad was determined to carry on.

It was snowing when we set off and still snowing a later as we

Sky burial

Historically, only lamas and other people of importance were cremated. In Tibet, where the wood required for funeral pyres is scarce, it was common practice for the dead bodies of less venerable human beings to be cut open and left at sky burial sites (also known as charnel grounds) to be eaten by animals, particularly vultures.

For Buddhists, who believe in the transmigration of spirits, the concept of an 'empty' human corpse providing food for other living beings fits well with their compassionate ideals.

crossed a bridge covered in prayer flags that marked the start of pass itself. For the next six hours, we walked uphill. My body felt heavy and my footsteps were slow, and it wasn't long before Chad was really struggling. Every time I glanced at Dorgee, he was watching us. And although I carried Chad's camera to try to make things a bit easier for him, I was as worried by his condition as Dorgee obviously was.

About halfway up the high pass, we stopped at a sky burial site, which is one of the last vantage points from which Mount Kailash is visible. After the Cultural Revolution in 1969, sky burial was banned for several years by the Chinese government, for health and hygiene reasons. But the practice continued in rural areas and in Tibet until some 20–30 years ago, when there was a drastic decline in the population of vultures. Without the vultures, the purpose of sky burial was lost and it is now rarely practiced. Today, instead of leaving bodies at sites like the one below the Dromla Pass, people bring clothing and other personal items that belonged to the deceased.

As we left the sky burial site, the thin snowfall exploded into a full-blown storm. As clouds and fog rolled across the mountains, the visibility reduced steadily until I could barely see my hand in front of my face. I didn't know where my breaking point was, but, at that moment, I knew I was pretty close to it. Even if my body does break, I told myself, I'm not giving up.

It can be depressing lying in a tent at night with nothing to focus

Decline in the population of vultures

Within a decade of the early 1990s, the numbers of vultures in India and south Asia reduced drastically. Several species that had previously been abundant became critically endangered.

After extensive research, the cause was identified as the painkiller diclofenac, which is commonly used in veterinary practice, and often given to dying patients in hospitals. The drug caused irreversible kidney damage in vultures that fed on the corpses of treated livestock.

on except your emotions. It's far more depressing to be ascending a high pass after walking for three hours, knowing there might be six more hours of walking ahead of you. But feeling sorry for yourself isn't going to help. The equation is simple: if you don't keep moving—however slow your pace—you'll die. That knowledge was all the incentive I needed to keep dragging my feet through the steadily deepening snow. Dorgee's cheerful encouragement helped too. 'Okay Boss?' he asked at regular intervals. 'Okay,' I would always answer. And, despite the unrelenting cold, the apparently negligible amount of oxygen contained in the small amount of air I did manage to draw down into my lungs, and the dull heaviness of my limbs, I *was* okay, not least because I was proud of what I was doing.

To want to do something so incredibly difficult, something most (sane) people wouldn't even attempt to do, perhaps there has to be a part of you that's not quite right. I was excited by the challenge. On Minya Konka, it was the rain; on Amne Machin, the sun; and on Mount Kailash, the snow and the altitude were the adversaries we had to face. I had known before we set out on the first trek several weeks earlier that each journey would bring different challenges: I just didn't know what those challenges would be, or whether I would be able to cope with them.

It helped that there weren't any moments on any of the treks when I was afraid for my life. I may not know exactly where the limits of my endurance lie, but I have a rough idea. I don't want to attempt to ice-climb Everest, for example, and risk being crushed by a glacier. I don't want to do handstands on the top of 40-story buildings. I'm not an adrenalin junkie. For me, it's all about adventure with a purpose and about pushing—not killing—myself.

I saw men and women, young and old, performing the *kora* at Mount Kailash. Their sole, shared, purpose in treading such an arduous path with dogged determination was to satisfy their religious beliefs. And although I don't share those beliefs, I found their spirit and the simplicity of their pilgrimage both motivating and inspiring. To do what they were doing requires a mentality very similar to that needed to play competitive sports.

My dad was an Olympic athlete who played in the Canadian water polo team in Munich in 1972. And I've played basketball almost my entire life. So I grew up with an understanding of what it takes to be a successful sportsman. During a basketball game, there are moments when you have to rise up and either shoot the ball or stop some guy on the opposing team from scoring. It's in those brief, crucial moments when your preparation, training, mental state, and physicality all have to come together so that you can meet the challenge and ensure victory for *your* team. When I stopped playing college basketball—because I wasn't good enough to play professionally—it left a huge void in my life. I guess I was looking for something to fill that void when I went to China for the first time in 2001. And what I discovered there was mountain trekking.

To trek around the sacred mountains, I needed to be physically fit—although, in fact, I had little time to prepare for each journey. And I needed to be psychologically prepared for the dark moments I knew would come. When those dark moments did arrive, I would think, 'Am I going to shrivel up and go home, or am I going to power through, deal with it, and carry on?' By the time we were ascending to the Dromla Pass, shriveling up and going home wasn't even an option. I was pumped up and ready for whatever nature planned to throw at me.

That day, as I hauled my aching body through the snow, I shook the hands of the people who overtook me—the tortoise to their hares. And I found myself smiling, because suddenly I knew that, as long as I didn't twist an ankle or break a leg, I would complete the journey I'd set out on. In my own moment of enlightenment, I realized that what I was doing was a metaphor for what I needed to do in every aspect of my life. Whatever 'mountains' I had to climb, however difficult the paths I had to tread, I *had* to keep moving forward. It didn't matter if the progress I made was slow and ponderous. As long as I didn't allow myself to be disheartened or distracted when the going got really tough, I would eventually reach my goal, whatever it might be.

Unfortunately, while I was having my epiphany, Chad was still feeling ill and was struggling to keep going. When the camera battery faded just before we reached the high pass, I noticed him fumbling with frozen fingers to change it.

By the time we were within a few meters of the high pass, the snow was falling thick and fast and we were walking so slowly we barely seemed to be moving at all. Suddenly, a guy strode past us wearing a long-sleeved polo shirt, canvas shoes, thin black pants, and a sun hat. He smiled as he overtook us. Then he left us in his cheerful wake, the sleeve of the warm jacket that was poking out of his backpack bouncing in time with his departing footsteps.

Maybe sensing our rapidly ebbing confidence, Dorgee assured us that it's never as cold in September as it was that day. 'It does snow at this time of year,' he told us. 'But it's warmer. This is the worst trip I have ever done.'

It was still snowing when we reached the high pass, where the ground was slushy and slippery. Ignoring our discomfort, we stayed there for about an hour and got some good film footage. But I was becoming increasingly worried about Chad, and my concern was exacerbated when he threw up shortly after we began our descent on the other side.

Our campsite that night was in a valley near a river. The wind hadn't let up all day and the sun had remained wrapped in thick, snow-laden clouds that absorbed its warmth and seemed to envelop the whole world. By the time we had put up our tents, I'd had enough of the cold. Dorgee brought me some bread and cheese, which I ate in my tent while the snow turned to hail and the wind howled across the valley. I stayed in my tent to do my video diary, which Chad filmed from inside his. Then I crawled into my sleeping bag and surrendered at last to the profound weariness I had been fighting all day.

When I opened my eyes on day four—day nine since we left Shanghai—the hail was still falling like bullets from a uniformly gray sky. The hail turned to snow not long after I stepped out of my tent. It was another cold start to what promised to be another bleak day. Despite the weather, I felt better than I had done the night before, and, more importantly, so did Chad. Each time it happened—which it did almost every day—I was always surprised by our ability to hit rock bottom and then bounce back again. However miserable and down-hearted I was when I went to bed, and however poorly I slept, I always seemed to wake up feeling optimistic, convinced that, today, everything would be all right.

By day four, we were back in the land of motor vehicles—of nomads driving trucks and motorbikes. We gave our remaining provisions—mostly oatmeal, chocolate, cheese, and yak meat—to some pilgrims who were camped in nomad huts on the banks of the river. Then Chad and I left Dorgee and the guides to pack up the animals and got back on the trail. At 4988 m (16,365 ft) ASL, well below the high pass, it was much easier to breathe there and, powered by a sudden sense of exuberance, I set off at a jog.

We had agreed to wait for the others at a teahouse about an hour and a half's walk from the campsite. It was still snowing when we got there and it felt good to take off our jackets, hats, and gloves while we warmed ourselves by the stove. We waited there for an hour, drinking hot water to rehydrate ourselves as rapidly as possible. By the time Dorgee and the other guides arrived, the snow had almost stopped and they decided we should continue on to the end of the trail.

It was a long walk, mostly downhill on gently sloping ground that was frozen and therefore not slippery under foot. Fortunately, Chad was on the road to a full recovery and he shared my anxiety to push on to Darchen so that we wouldn't have to camp for another night. Half an hour after we left the teahouse, the snow started to fall again and the temperature plummeted. It felt like the final test, as if nature and the gods of the mountain were reminding us that they were still in control.

We were walking through the valley, the end of our journey almost within our grasp, when we came to a particularly pronounced bend in the winding glacial river. As we rounded it, the sun broke through the clouds and I climbed up onto some rocks to take a photograph of the mountains behind us. During my career as a photographer, I've taken a lot of photographs from dizzying heights—standing on mountains as well as crouched precariously on skyscrapers in the process of construction. But I've never been as uneasy as I was at that moment, and I was grateful for Chad's steadying hand while I risked life and limb for some great shots.

Exhausted but triumphant, we arrived at the last teahouse on the trail. We didn't know the teahouse marked the end of our trek until we saw the bus that had taken us to the start of our journey four days earlier and would now drive us back to Darchen. Normally, even with their yaks and donkeys, the guides walked much faster than we did. On that occasion, however, fueled by a desire to get out of the cold, Chad and I were at least half an hour ahead of them. The bus driver was happy to wait, and we were happy to pass the time in the warm teahouse, drinking tea and eating noodles. When the others arrived, we did some filming, settled up with the guides, loaded our bags onto the bus, and headed back to Darchen to close the circle of our *kora*.

By the end of our third journey, I had begun to feel that I was experiencing something I couldn't quantify or even fully explain. Trekking in the sacred mountains seemed to have insinuated itself into my life and had become, quite simply, what I did.

I had waited 12 years to visit Mount Kailash. When I finally got there, it turned out to be the toughest of the three treks we had done so far. Each time I thought, '*This* one is the hardest one of all.' But on Mount Kailash I felt more mind-numbingly cold than I've ever felt in my life, before or since. Even when it snowed, nothing was damp. When snow hit you, it didn't turn to water and soak into your clothes. It fell to the ground, still snow, because, like everything else in that bleak, windswept environment, there was no warmth in your body to melt it.

I'm sure conditions on Everest, in the Arctic or Antarctic are far worse than on Mount Kailash. But maybe there's a point at which you can't feel any colder, no matter how much lower the temperature drops. If there is, I think I reached my own personal 'state of maximum coldness' on that trip.

Of the tourists and pilgrims who set off at the same time as we did, some had turned back, some had fallen behind, and some had surged ahead. It was partly because of the people we met—the two brothers, the pilgrims doing prostrations, the guy striding through the high pass in shirt sleeves and canvas shoes—that Mount Kailash provided me with a moment of enlightenment. And it was partly because, this time, I really was pushed to the limits of my endurance. Maybe the fact that the journey had been so grueling made the achievement seem even greater. I returned to Shanghai with a sense that I had done something special.

I had been inspired by the pilgrims I had encountered on the mountain. If my experience inspired just one person to do something they had always wanted to do—or maybe something they hadn't imagined would ever be possible—all the hardship and discomfort would have been worthwhile.

Mount Kailash. Ice-cold water cascades from the waterfall on the left into one of the many rivers that flow through the valleys surrounding the mountain.

Mount Kailash. The sunlit snow on the west face of the mountain peak contrasts sharply with the dark, jagged rocks beneath it.

Mount Kailash. The only place to camp on this occasion is on rough, stone-covered ground under the north face of the mountain.

Mount Kailash. Packing up camp is a dismal process in the bitter cold of the early morning on what turns out to be the toughest day of the trek as we ascend to the Shula Pass.

Mount Kailash. The clouds roll in and the snow starts to fall as we begin the ascent to the Shula Pass.

Mount Kailash. On the way up to the Shula Pass, the midway point of the trek is marked by a heavy snowstorm.

Mount Kailash. More storm clouds cover the mountains as we descend on the other side of the Shula Pass.

Mount Kailash. Pilgrims make their way along the trail around the eastern side of the sacred mountain.

Kawa Karpo. Corn has been hung out to dry on the balcony of one of the old wooden houses in the village of Yongtsa, where we began our trek around the mountain.

Kawa Karpo. Our guide and translator, Dorgee, and I stop for a drink at one of the small shops along the route on the first day of the fourth, and last, mountain trek.

Kawa Karpo. Incredible mountain scenery surrounds our camp on high-altitude grassland in the last valley before the high pass.

Kawa Karpo. Pilgrims who have stayed overnight in a teahouse on their *kora* around the sacred mountain huddle close to the stove where water is being boiled for yak-butter tea.

Kawa Karpo. There are small shops like this one at intervals along the route selling high-carb drinks, sweets, alcohol, and other 'essential' provisions to fortify weary pilgrims and other travelers.

Kawa Karpo. Prayer flags mark the start of the Duoke La Pass, on the border between the province of Tibet and the province of Yunnan.

Kawa Karpo. Looking back down the trail after a grueling ascent to the Duoke La Pass at 16,076 ft (4900 m) above sea level.

Kawa Karpo. In the later stages of our trek, we encountered some young Tibetan boys ducking and weaving their way on motorcycles through strands of prayer flags on an impossibly narrow path at the very edge of the mountain.

Kawa Karpo. On the other side of the high pass, the trail continues, descending now towards the Nujiang River in Tibet.

Kawa Karpo. Towards the end of the trek, the landscape changed again and we entered a remote region of dust-brown mountains and glacial blue rivers, with the occasional small group of houses above cultivated terraces.

Kawa Karpo. Corn and other recently harvested crops are laid out to dry on the rooftops of homes in Kelbu village.

Kawa Karpo. Two young inhabitants of Kelbu village stop to have their photograph taken.

Kawa Karpo. Preparing to leave the guesthouse in Kelbu village before setting off for the Shula Pass, which would be the last pass on the last of my four treks.

Kawa Karpo. An example of what most dinners are like up on the Tibetan Plateau while trekking. A small bowl of cabbage, potato and rice.

Kawa Karpo. Just making it to the top of the Shu La Pass was a victory in itself. It marked the end of an incredibly challenging day.

Kawa Karpo. A final photograph taken with the ever-cheerful Dorgee (far left) and the guides who helped me to complete my fourth and final trek around some of the sacred mountains of China.

The best months to travel to Mount Kailash are July and August.

The trek around Mount Kailash presents a significant physical and psychological challenge as well as providing a reflective experience.

This 2–5-day trek begins and ends in the village of Darchen (15,010 ft/4575 m) in Tibet Autonomous Region.

After completing the trek around the mountain, most people drive from Darchen to Lake Manasarovar, where they spend a night or two before continuing on to Lhasa. If you opt to fly back to Lhasa, you'll then have to make the 2-hour drive north to the airport in Ali. If you decide to drive to Lhasa, you could make a detour en route to Everest Base Camp.

How to Get to Mount Kailash

Fly to Lhasa Gonggar Airport in Tibet Autonomous Region, China.

Hire a driver and car for the 3-day drive west to Darchen, stopping overnight in the towns of Xigaze (12,795 ft/3900 m) and Lhatse (13,287 ft/4050 m).

Alternatively, you can fly from Lhasa to Ali's Ngari Gunsa Airport, on the one, 90-minute, flight per week.

When you arrive at Darchen, you can hire guides, cooks, and yaks. Your guides will organize the necessary permits.

Darchen is a friendly place. Take advantage of its teahouses to get one last good meal before you set out.

Be sure to stock up on provisions in the well-stocked Darchen market.

Potential Costs

For non-Chinese-passport holders, traveling in Tibet Autonomous Region is *expensive*!

The following costs are based on the assumption that you are traveling alone, rather than in a tour group, and were correct in October 2013, when US$1 = 6.15 Yuan.

Flight Chengdu to Lhasa: 1500 Yuan

Flight from Lhasa to Ali: 2560 Yuan

Cost of car, driver and guides for drive from Ngari Gunsa Airport in Ali to Lhasa, from there to Lake Manasarovar, then to Mount Kailash, and back to the airport in Ali, plus guides for 3 days in Lhasa, for time spent at the lake and for the trek around the

mountain, plus all permits required for visiting and trekking in
the region: 40,000 Yuan
Cost per yak/donkey: 250 Yuan per day
Cost per yak/donkey handler/guide/cook: 200 Yuan per day
Cost of food: budget for 200–300 Yuan per person per day
Flights from Ali to Lhasa to Chengdu: 4060 Yuan
Note. Costs might fluctuate during high season. Expect to pay more
with a tour group.

How I Completed this Trek
I flew from Shanghai to Chengdu to Lhasa to Ali.
I arranged for a driver and car to pick us up at Ngari Gunsa Airport
in Ali, and drive us to Darchen, where I applied for the necessary
permits and organized the 2 guides with 3 yaks and 1 donkey we
needed for the trek around Mount Kailash.
At the end of the trek, I hired another car and driver to take us back
to the airport in Ali.
I flew from Ali to Lhasa to Chengdu to Shanghai.

Important note. You should be sure to consult a physician before
attempting any high-altitude trekking. Many pilgrims and travelers
to these regions die each year because of health problems and lack
of preparedness. The risks are REAL.

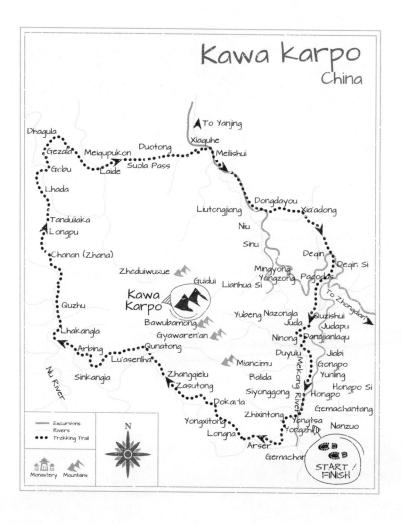

Kawa Karpo
China

To Yanjing

Dhagula
Gezala
Gebu
Duotong
Meiqupukon
Laide
Suola Pass
Xiaquhe
Meilishui
Lhada
Tanduilaka
Longpu
Dongdayou
Liutongjiang
Xia'adong
Niu
Sinu
Deqin
Deqin Si
Chanan (Zhana)
Zhaduiwuxue
Guidui
Mingyong
Yongzong
Pagodas
To Zhongdian
Kawa
Karpo
Lianhua Si
Quzhu
Bawubamong
Gyawaren'an
Yubeng
Nazongla
Juda
Quzishui
Judapu
Lhakangla
Arbing
Qunatong
Lu'asenlha
Ninong
Dangjianlaqu
Jiabi
Gongpo
Yunling
Hongpo Si
Sinkangla
Miancimu
Balida
Duyulu
Nu River
Zhangqielu
Zasutong
Siyonggong
Hongpo
Gemachantang
Pokarla
Zhixintong
Yangtsa
Nanzuo
Yongxitong
Longna
Arser
Yongzhilu
Gernachar
START /
FINISH

Excursions
Rivers
Trekking Trail

N

Monastery   Mountains

Kawa Karpo

Kawa Karpo—also known as Kawagarbo—is part of the Meili massif of the extensive Hengduan Mountain range on the eastern edge of the Tibetan Plateau. With an elevation of 6740 m (22,113 ft) above sea level (ASL), it is the highest mountain in Yunnan Province. The Mingyong Glacier that currently descends on the east face of Kawa Karpo to the Mekong River valley is rapidly retreating, apparently as a result of climate change.

Tibetan Buddhists believe that the warrior god Kawagarbo resides at the top of the mountain and that if the summit were to be scaled, he would leave and many disasters would follow. However, despite the objections of local people, attempts have been made to climb Kawa Karpo. The first recorded attempt was by Japanese climbers in 1987. In 1991, all 17 members of a combined group of Japanese and Chinese climbers were killed in an avalanche not far from the summit. In 1996, another group from Japan made an unsuccessful attempt. In 2001, the local government banned the climbing of Kawa Karpo, on cultural and religious grounds.

/ 8 \

On 22 October 2013, I flew with Chad from Shanghai to Kunming and then on to Shangri-La. The average temperature in Shanghai in October is 20°C (68°F). At 3770 m (12,369 ft) above sea level, Shangri-La is below freezing at night. It was windy, too, when we arrived at midnight. Dorgee, who was our fixer and translator on the trek to Mount Kailash, had agreed to come with us again and he met us at the airport.

The next morning, we were picked up at the hotel by the driver Dorgee had hired to drive us to the village of Deqen, where we would start the trek. It was raining when we set off on the 175 km (108 mile) journey, which took us nearly seven hours on roads that twisted and turned through the mountains like the sinewy contours of a writhing snake.

I had returned to Shanghai from the US just four days before leaving again to fly to Shangri-La. They were days I wanted to spend with my family, but most of my time was occupied by tedious last-minute planning. As we crawled slowly along the switchback roads in that interminable drive through the mountains, I was worrying about the things that can't be planned for, particularly the weather. After walking in a snowstorm for three days at Mount Kailash, I knew just how tough conditions could be.

Then the rain stopped, the sun came out, and I felt a sudden surge of excitement. Instantly, as if by the flick of a switch, all the mundane hassles involved in getting ourselves and our excess baggage from Shanghai to Shangri-La were relegated to the past. Once again, I was an explorer setting out on a new adventure.

The area we were heading for isn't reliably charted—there were two places labeled as Deqen on Google Maps. There is some infor-

Shangri-La

The town of Zhongdian in northwestern Yunnan Province was once a stop-off point on the southern Silk Road. In 2001, in an attempt to boost tourism, it was renamed Shangri-La, the name of the earthly paradise depicted in the 1930s' novel *Lost Horizon*, by the British author James Hilton.

The book—which was subsequently made into a movie—was said to have been at least partly inspired by Joseph Rock's articles for *National Geographic* about his explorations in Tibet.

mation about it in old trekking books, but it's confusing. So people tend to travel on package tours with tour guides in the more remote parts of rural China. If you want to go it alone, you have to be prepared to work it out when you get there.

The road to Deqen cut through some amazing mountain scenery. But it was a long, bumpy ride and I was glad when we arrived. We booked into a hotel that has a roof-top terrace and a magnificent view of the mountain. Or so we were told. When we went up to the terrace the next morning, all we could see were clouds. It was an unwelcome reminder that, at that time of year particularly, the clouds might not disperse for days and then we wouldn't see the sacred mountain at all. It had happened when I visited Kawa Karpo for the first time five years ago when trekking with a friend. We walked for at least half the journey in rain, and even when it stopped, the clouds hung over all the mountains like an opaque gray curtain.

We stayed at a guesthouse after completing the trek on that occasion, where we met an older couple who had turned back after walking for a couple of hours in the rain. I was shocked to think that they had spent time and money on all the planning and preparation, traveled all the way from Western Europe, and then abandoned an eight-day trek simply because it rained for a while on the first day. I think they felt a bit stupid after they told us, and they were right to feel embarrassed. If it's raining when you set out, you have to believe it's going to stop—on the other side of the high pass, if not before. And if it doesn't stop raining, you don't stop walking. The only thing that should deter you from doing what you set out to do is the risk of injury. There's far more to be gained from walking in the mountains than the chance to see even the most spectacular view.

After a night in Deqen, we drove for an hour and a half along the Mekong River to the village of Yongtsa, where we would hire guides and a cook before starting the *kora*. We had ascended to a mountain pass the previous day, and then descended about 1300 m (4265 ft) by the time we arrived in Yongtsa. It seemed counterintuitive to be coming down before starting the trek. It was an introduction to the undulating path we would be following for the next few days.

In Yongtsa, I looked for a man called Sanjay Norbu, who, with his wife and brother, had been the guide on my previous visit to the mountain. The problem was, I couldn't remember where he lived. I asked people walking on the narrow village street if they knew him, and was beginning to give up any hope of finding him when I saw his wife. She recognized me, too, and told me that Norbu was on his way back from Deqen, where he had gone to buy cement for the new house they were building.

There are many skilled carpenters in Tibet and some of the village houses are beautiful. I think almost all the houses were made of wood the last time I was in Yongtsa. Now, there are several new cement buildings similar to those currently being constructed all over China. When you live in harsh conditions in a remote,

Shangri-La is destroyed by fire

In January 2014, less than three months after I visited it, the small mountain town of Shangri-La was devastated by fire.

Thousands of firefighters, police, and soldiers were deployed to fight the blaze. But, fanned by dry air and propelled by wind, the fire swept through the narrow alleyways of the old town, destroying hundreds of its ancient wooden buildings. Severe damage was also caused to the modern Chinese district that had been built around the old town.

Miraculously, there were no casualties among the town's 3000 inhabitants, according to official sources.

high-altitude region like the Tibetan Plateau, the choice between esthetics and the amenities available in modern houses probably isn't a very difficult one to make.

Norbu's wife took us to their little wooden house, where we drank tea and waited for Norbu. When he arrived, we reminisced about the trek we had done together. 'It was a good trip,' Norbu said. 'You had great spirit.'

'I'm doing it again,' I told him. 'We're leaving tomorrow. I would really like you to come with us. Can you make it?'

If you turned up at someone's house in the Western world and gave them 18 hours notice of what was likely to be a very demanding trek lasting for several days, they wouldn't take you seriously. Until very recently, before internet access and mobile phones became available in some areas of rural Tibet, 'turning up' was the only way of doing it. Unfortunately, it didn't work out on this occasion. Norbu couldn't come with us because he had hired men to help him build the new house. And his wife couldn't come either, because they now have a young son. I was sorry to be going without them, but it was good to see them again.

The last time I was in Yongtsa, there was no shortage of people ready and willing to act as guides and cooks on the *kora*. Now, mobile phones seem to be ubiquitous, but guides are hard to find. Norbu phoned some friends and three men turned up at the house a few minutes later. They talked at length, to each other and to Dorgee, but their discussions didn't seem to be reaching any conclusions. Eventually, I suggested to Dorgee that we should go outside and discuss our options.

While we were walking around the village, we talked to a few people, including one of the guides who came with me on the previous trek. But everyone wanted ridiculous sums of money—in most cases, four times what I paid before, and at least twice what it cost on the three mountain treks we had just completed. Maybe life in the village is more expensive than it used to be. Or maybe local people have discovered easier ways to earn a living. Whatever the reason, it seemed that they simply weren't interested in being guides any more.

We went back to Norbu's house and after more discussions, he phoned a tour operator who has a guesthouse in the village and organizes a lot of treks. It was about 15.00 when we carried our bags up the hill to the guesthouse. By the evening, the guy had found us three guides who were able to leave the next morning for the 240 km (149 mile) trek. But he couldn't find a cook.

We walked back down the hill to speak to Norbu again. Then he phoned a neighbor, who came to his house a few minutes later and seemed keen to come with us. The cook had her own cooking utensils and stores of food—bags of rice and noodles, vegetables, and preserved yak meat. So, after the business side of things had been agreed, we went with her to a small shop in the village to buy the few other items we would need.

It had been quite a stressful afternoon. But, as we trudged wearily up the hill to the guesthouse for the last time, it was a relief to know that it was all finally settled. Once again, Dorgee had been super-helpful, and I was glad we weren't going to have to spend another day in the village trying to work it all out.

The next morning, the sun was shining and the breakfast was great. I was enjoying my eggs, Tibetan bread, peanut butter, jam, and coffee when the guesthouse owner came into the dining room and told me, 'Your cook phoned and said she can't go with you.' Just as everything seemed to be going so well . . .

In fact, it wasn't that she *couldn't* go with us: she had decided she wanted more money. Apparently, news had reached the village of a Chinese group who would be arriving in a couple of days and who were offering to pay more. The guesthouse owner asked if I wanted to phone her back myself or if he should go and talk to her. 'There's no need for either of us to talk to her,' I said. 'We're going to load up the donkeys and go down to her house. We negotiated a price, she agreed to it, and we made a deal.'

The woman's house was close to the shop and it was part of our agreement that she would pack up all the food ready to be loaded onto the donkeys that morning. She knew we wouldn't be able to find another cook at such short notice, and I guess she thought that being in the possession of the food gave her additional bargaining power. She could think again.

'Don't contact her,' I insisted to the guesthouse owner. 'And don't pick up the phone if she calls. When we're ready to leave, we'll head down to her house, and she better be ready too.'

So that's what we did. We finished our breakfast, packed up all our gear, and then Chad, Dorgee, the three guides, five donkeys, and I walked down the hill to the woman's house. By the time we reached her door, she was packed and waiting for us. She didn't mention money and I didn't either. We both just acted as if nothing had ever been said. Unfortunately though, something like that sours the relationship right from the start. I don't really want someone on my team who tries to pull a trick like that at the eleventh hour. As things turned out, she did her best for us during the trek and she was a good cook.

I think what our cook attempted to do was unusual. The fact that most Tibetans aren't motivated by money is one of the factors that can make organizing anything in Tibet really frustrating. Obviously, it's a good thing in many respects. What it means, however, is that when you agree a price with someone for something that involves them turning up at a particular place at a particular time, they might not show up at all. They know that if they don't, they won't get paid, but they don't really care. Doing business in Tibet is a reminder that, rightly or wrongly, sometimes money really is what makes the world go round. If you don't have any financial incentive—bills to pay, kids to feed, clothe, and educate— you don't have any impelling reason to do the things you've said you would do.

I stopped a few meters along the trail and looked down at the village. The sun was shining, the sky was blue, and the air was warm. Finally, I was able to let go of all the anxieties of the 'set-up' and focus on the journey ahead.

We followed a glacial river on an almost vertical path through dense woodland for about six hours. Then the trees began to thin out and the temperature dropped. Above the tree-line, most of the summer vegetation had already succumbed to the freezing night-time temperatures. The sun wouldn't set until about 19.00, but it had already disappeared behind the mountains by 16.00. Half an hour later, it was too cold to be outside.

How many footsteps does it take to create a visible trail? I often wondered about all the people who had trod the path before me, some of them centuries earlier. Today, more than 20,000 pilgrims and tourists visit Kawa Karpo every year and teahouses have sprung up along the trail—some of them little more than loosely secured planks of wood topped by large plastic sheets—to provide them with food, drink, and somewhere warm to sleep.

For many people, doing a *kora* is a sociable as well as a spiritual experience, and the pilgrims who stay in the teahouses tend to talk and drink long into the night, which is why I preferred to camp. Despite telling our guides to bring tents, they only had sleeping bags. So they slept in teahouses every night and we set our tents nearby. We sat by the fire in a teahouse that first night to eat our meal of cabbage, potatoes, onions, red peppers, and rice. Then I fell asleep thinking about my family and about how much I was looking forward to completing the last trek and being at home with them again.

I woke up at about 03.00, feeling disorientated and needing to go to the bathroom. When I stepped out of the tent into the freezing night, I thought the sun was shining. Then I realized that the light was coming from the moon. Oblivious to the cold, I stood for a few seconds looking at the stars and at the silver-blue snow on the mountaintops. There are times when exhaustion and the physicality of what you're doing drive every thought from your mind. And there are rare moments when you see a landscape that is so awe inspiring that every difficult, miserable experience of every journey you have ever undertaken seems suddenly to have been worthwhile.

On the morning of the second day of the trek, we scuttled into the teahouse to eat our breakfast by the fire. A little while later, I was warm again, my stomach was full of food, and I felt ready to take on whatever the day threw at me.

We packed up our bags, loaded them onto the donkeys, and left the campsite at 09.30. The sun was still low in the sky behind the mountains and there was little light in the valley. But our guides were adamant that we had to set off early. To reach the Duoke La Pass, at 4900 m (16,076 ft), we were facing a 1400 meter (4593 ft) ascent. If the sun disappeared again before we completed the descent into the valley on the other side, we would run the risk of having to walk in the dark.

I was sweating profusely by the time we reached the last teahouse before the high pass. I bought some peach juice and Snickers bars for quick refueling on the trail ahead, then changed my wet shirt and put on my warm North Face jacket and gloves. Not long after we set off again, we crossed a bridge and began an almost vertical climb to a ridge where the landscape was almost devoid of trees and where even the toughest grass struggled to grow.

We were already well above the tree line that day when we stopped to rest for a few minutes. The wind was vicious and I crouched behind a rock to try to shelter from it while I ate tuna straight out the can using a couple of twigs as makeshift chopsticks.

Some people take a shorter, almost vertical path up to the Duoke La Pass. But I felt weaker than I had done on the three preceding journeys and I knew it would be beyond my capabilities. Perhaps my energy had been sapped by the never-ending ascents and descents. Or maybe I was simply suffering from cumulative exhaustion. Whatever the cause of my acute weariness, we took the longer, less precipitous, switchback path. Even then, the wind that blew straight down the mountain kept pushing me back like some solid but invisible force.

We did some filming on the high pass and I put up some of the prayer flags Dorgee had brought with him. I would have liked to have stayed there longer, particularly after all the effort that had been involved in getting there. It was the cold that defeated me in the end. After 30 minutes, my fingers and toes were numb and I was beginning to feel the effects of exposure. So we followed the donkeys' tracks and began a vertical zigzag descent along a thousand switchbacks that were even more difficult and exhausting to negotiate than the ones on the way up.

Just as I was beginning to wonder if I was going to make it, we met a group of laughing, chattering women. They had worked on the land throughout the spring and summer, they told us. But now that it was frozen and unproductive, they were doing a *kora* together. They were clearly having a very good time and their cheerful companionship gave me the boost I needed to stumble on down the river valley.

Eventually, we descended back to the tree-line again and walked for a while through mixed woodland. Many of the deciduous trees had lost already their leaves and many of them had branches draped with thick strands of silvery-green lichen. We set our camp near the river, at 3900 m (12,795 ft) and then sat by the fire in a teahouse. I was too tired to eat. So, after doing my video diary, I went straight to bed, leaving Chad to film the sunset.

In fact, Chad seemed to have coped much better than me with the day's exertions. Not long after we stopped walking, the reason for my inordinate struggle became apparent and I realized I felt quite ill. I hadn't eaten anything all day except oatmeal, Snickers bars, and tuna, all of which Chad had eaten too. Then I remembered that, just as we were about to set out that morning, I had returned to the teahouse to fill my flask with boiled drinking water. Perhaps I had taken it from the wrong container. I was glad that my 'stomach issue' hadn't reached its peak while we were still walking. It was about to become the least of my problems.

Kawa Karpo sits on the border between the provinces of Yunnan and Tibet, a border we crossed when we came over through the Duoke La Pass. We weren't going to be in Tibet for very long. The trail continued along the Nujiang River for a two days before veering off into the mountain again, up to another high pass, then back into Yunnan and down to the Mekong River. We hadn't known before we set out that foreigners aren't allowed to be in this part of Tibet—even for the short distance involved—without permits, which we didn't have. Nor had I known that there is now a road linking the villages along the Nujiang River and that on the road there are roadblocks manned by police specifically on the look-out for foreigners doing the trek around the mountain.

We were descending from the Duoke La Pass when our guides mentioned the permits, the road, and the roadblocks, and asked what we were planning to do. Hundreds of foreign tourists do the trek around Kawa Karpo every year, so I couldn't believe there would really be a problem. But the guides were obviously anxious.

'We don't want to get busted,' they told us. 'We don't want to get into trouble and be turned back.'

That's when it dawned on me that there was a very distinct possibility we weren't going to be able to finish our fourth and final trek in the sacred mountains. It was a thought that would have stopped me sleeping on any other night. On that particular night, however, I expected to be kept awake by physiological problems.

/ 9 \

I had a surprisingly good sleep and woke up the next morning feeling almost well again. We packed up our tents, ate our breakfast in the teahouse, and started walking just as the sun appeared above the mountains, spreading color across the monochrome landscape.

We walked downhill for most of the morning, sometimes on muddy ground, following the river through the forest. Around midday, we stopped at a teahouse for a brief rest and I had a competition with Chad to see who could get an empty plastic bottle into a garbage can, which Chad won by an impressive margin. My university basketball coach would have been disappointed in me.

It's strange how something as simple as laughing at a stupid game can change your mental state. Despite the beautiful landscape, the walking that morning had been hard slog. But I set off from the teahouse feeling cheerful.

After a couple of hours, the path narrowed and we were forced to negotiate some steep drops. There had been several landslides on the trail and for some of the time we were walking on scree, which skittered and shifted underfoot before clattering down the slope. We continued to follow the contours of the undulating landscape and then ascended to another mountain pass on a tree-covered ridge.

The trail at the pass was almost obliterated by prayer flags, some of them brilliant shades of red, blue, yellow, and green, others bleached and faded by the sun, which shone that day in an almost cloudless sky. In fact, there were so many flags that, in some places, they completely obscured the path on strands that were too dense to fight your way through and too wide to be able to walk around.

It was pilgrim season in Tibet, the time when, having harvested their crops and closed up their farms for the winter, farmers are able to visit holy sites like the sacred mountain of Kawa Karpo. We arrived at the pass at the same time as several cheerful pilgrims, who thanked me as I lifted up some of the heavy strands of flags just high enough for them to be able to duck underneath. I had to call Dorgee's name several times before he finally emerged from the tangled mass of prayer flags, breathless and with his sunglasses askew. We were ahead of the donkeys by then, and I couldn't imagine how they would negotiate that section of the path.

Every rock and every inch of the ground around and underneath the flags was covered in a thick layer of tsampa. 'Our spirits will come here after we die,' one of the pilgrims told Dorgee. 'And at that time we will need food. So that's why we are leaving tsampa here now.' They were leaving clothing too, laying hats, jackets, and shirts on the rocks and throwing them up into the branches of trees from which there already dangled many similar items.

Interacting with the pilgrims at that pass was a very special, uplifting experience that left me feeling optimistic and put the spring back into my previously flagging footsteps.

At the next teahouse, there were several men with motorcycles hanging around, waiting to transport pilgrims further along the trail. It was an abrupt and, for me, premature reintroduction to the modern world. The terrain was rough for any vehicle and the idea of pilgrims doing part of the *kora* by motorcycle taxi seemed bizarre. There hadn't been any teahouses at all last time I was on the mountain. I guess it isn't only in the cities that life moves on, or where one person's revered tradition is another's business opportunity. In fact, arriving at that teahouse marked the point at which the whole expedition became quite strange.

We didn't stop there; we carried on and set our camp near the next teahouse, at 2700 m (8858 ft) ASL. It was difficult to maintain any sense of continuity with the past when motorcycles were constantly nudging us out of the way on the narrow trail. And it was even more difficult when I could hear them zipping through the trees next to our campsite for most of the night. The positive feeling I'd had since talking to pilgrims at the pass quickly faded to neutral, at best.

Nujiang River

The Nujiang River (known in Burmese as the Salween) rises in the Qinghai Mountains on the Tibetan Plateau and extends for 2815 km (1749 miles) through China, Burma and Thailand to the Andaman Sea in Southeast Asia. Its source is close to the headwaters of the Mekong and Yangtze rivers.

The Nujiang is one of the longest, undammed, free-flowing rivers in the world. During the last few years, logging has damaged its ecology and there is currently opposition on environmental grounds to numerous plans to dam the river in China.

Nu Jiang means 'Angry River' in Chinese, although it actually gets its name from a local tribe of people called the Nu.

During the Second World War, allied forces under an American commander took part in the Salween Campaign, which was launched to liberate Japanese-occupied China and reopen the recently constructed Burma Road, which crosses the river at what in 1944 was the strategically important Huitong Bridge.

While we were eating our meal that evening, our guides started talking again about the checkpoints along the Nujiang River. They told us they had been turned back with foreigners on previous occasions and they asked us again what plans we had for getting through. The answer was 'None', and I went to bed that night feeling unsettled.

As far as I was concerned, going back around the mountain, through the Duoke La Pass to Yongtsa village without finishing what we set out to do simply wasn't an option. The trouble was, if we were stopped at a checkpoint—which, according to our guides, would almost certainly happen—that was exactly what we were going to have to do.

I didn't feel any less apprehensive when I woke up early the next morning. That day's trekking would take us up to another small mountain pass and then down the other side to a village on the river. We packed up all the gear, then Chad and I discussed our options.

As well as transporting pilgrims, the motorcyclists carry information back and forth along the trail. In the teahouse the previous evening, a couple of them mentioned to our guides that there were a lot of police in the village. Apparently, a group of 15 Korean trekkers that came through a few weeks earlier were sent back south along the Nujiang River to Gongshan—which is in Yunnan Province and in completely the wrong direction for continuing the trek around the mountain. The consensus seemed to be that if we went into the village, we would be busted too.

It was incredibly frustrating. I didn't *want* to leave Yunnan and travel into Tibet Autonomous Region—both of which are provinces within the People's Republic of China. I was simply following the route of the *kora*. And I didn't know we needed permits. If they sold them in Yongtsa village—which seems the obvious place, as it's where everyone starts the trek—I would gladly have paid whatever they cost. But, apparently, the only place you can buy them is in Lhasa—which is about 1000 km (621 miles) west of where we were.

Going forward would clearly be fraught with difficulties. Going back wasn't an option I was prepared to consider. So what *were* we going to do?

The area of the Nujiang River valley we were heading for is currently undergoing a process of development and several villages are already linked by a recently constructed road. We had to work out how to travel along that road and then pick up the trail on the mountain without being stopped by the police. Eventually, a plan was hatched. We would walk up to the next small pass and down the other side. Then we would wait until dark before entering the first village, where some guys with motorcycles would drive us along the road and take us back into the mountains to pick up the trail again.

I didn't want Dorgee to get into any trouble on our behalf, so Chad and I kept him out of our discussions and made all the arrangements directly with the men.

'It will be fine,' one of them told us. 'You are just a day behind an Italian who a friend of ours took through without any problems.'

I knew that might or might not be true—after all, they were selling their services, so they had every reason to want to convince us that everything would be okay. True or not, however, the bottom line was that, after what felt like a very long and exhausting race, I was perilously close to falling at the final hurdle. If the plan wasn't successful, I would not be able to complete the treks or the documentary I had set out to make.

There were lots of reasons, conscious and subconscious, why I had wanted to trek in the sacred mountains—to commune with nature, find myself, see the bigger picture, broaden my horizons, extend the limits of my endurance . . . I hated the fact that, at best, it was going to end with us sneaking around under the cover of darkness while trying to avoid the police. Quite apart from the filming aspect, I felt that I *had* to finish this last journey, for some personal reason I didn't fully comprehend.

The road that now exists along the Nujiang River is actually part of the *kora* itself, although, according to our guides, no one does the full *kora* of Kawa Karpo anymore. Apparently, most people start at Yongtsa village and go up to the Duoke La Pass, as we did. But then they stop walking—less than halfway round—and take a minibus along the road back to Deqen. I guess it depends on why you're doing it.

For me, it was a personal challenge, as well as an opportunity to share the magnificence of the sacred mountains with people who might be inspired by my experience to have an adventure of their own. Perhaps because my motivation wasn't religious or social, I had a slightly different perspective from that of the pilgrims. On the other hand, I can't help thinking that doing even part of a *kora* in a bus or on the back of a motorcycle is rather defeating the meditative purpose and not quite what the gods or Buddha had in mind.

For Chad and me, there didn't seem to be any alternative other than to go along with the plan suggested. Once the decision had been made, we headed up to the mountain pass—now almost the only people still on foot. After doing some filming, we descended towards the riverside village and the next phase of our journey. I wasn't looking forward to it at all. Quite apart from the risk we would be taking by playing cat and mouse with the authorities—which was something I really didn't want to do—there would be real danger involved in walking down to the village in the dark on a narrow mountain trail with a steep drop on either side.

It was heavy going descending from the pass on ground rendered unstable by loose stones and broken fragments of rock. By the time we stopped to wait for darkness to fall, my knees and hamstrings ached, my heels were rubbed raw, and it felt as though the soles of my feet were on fire. It was 15.00, which meant we had a few hours to kill before nightfall.

It hadn't been dark for very long when we heard the sound of a single motorcycle engine, distantly at first and then growing louder as it came closer. The guy who stopped beside us probably meant to be reassuring when he said, 'You can walk down to the village. The police won't bother you now that it's dark. When you get there, two of my friends will be waiting for you. Wear your hats and cover your faces with scarves so no one can see you're foreigners. And don't speak—in English or Chinese—because that will certainly give you away.'

Some people might get a buzz from sneaking through the shadows with their collars turned up and their faces covered, like characters out of a spy movie. It made me feel sick with anxiety.

Dorgee wasn't breaking any law, so when we got down to the village, he walked, unmasked, ahead of us. There were quite a few people around, going about their own, legitimate, business. Even though they appeared not to be very interested in what we were doing, I was convinced that someone's suspicions would be raised by the sight of Chad and me loitering in the shadows with scarves covering our faces like highwaymen or bank robbers. What was worrying me even more was the possibility that we were being set up—for reasons I was too stressed and jittery to try to work out.

When we reached a bridge, we stopped under its stone arch and I tried to shake some of the tension out of my shoulders. We'd been standing there for just a couple of minutes when I heard a low whistle and saw someone beckoning to us. If I was a religious man, I would definitely have been praying as we ran silently across the road to what appeared to be a motorcycle taxi hangout.

I couldn't understand the whispered exchanges and I hated not knowing what was going on. The knot in my stomach seemed to be getting tighter with every anxious second that passed. Even though Chad's face was covered too, I could tell he was feeling equally apprehensive. Despite the risk we were taking and the precariousness of our situation, I also suspected he was wishing he could film our reluctant adventure.

Suddenly, I was on the back of a motorbike being driven by a lad of about 17 years old in total darkness along a twisting, turning mountain road that neither of us could actually see. As we bounced through water, gravel, dust, and dirt that blew up into my face in the wake of every car that passed, I clung on to that kid as though my life depended on him—which, in fact, in did.

The motorcycle wasn't designed for a 6-foot pillion passenger. It would have been uncomfortable even if I hadn't been forced to sit with my knees almost touching my chin. We had been driving for about an hour and a half when we stopped at the side of the road. A few seconds later, the motorcycles carrying Chad and Dorgee pulled in behind us. Dorgee wasn't doing anything wrong and didn't have to hide from the authorities; he traveled with us so that he could translate if the need arose.

'We're coming up to the first checkpoint,' my driver said. 'There's a police station and a barrier across the road. It's just a steel chain. So you can drive right underneath it on a motorbike.'

It didn't sound like a foolproof plan. Didn't the police have motorbikes too, and fast cars? Wouldn't they come after us? Or did they just ignore motorcyclists who dodged under the barrier without stopping? It was too late to ask those and the many other questions that sprang immediately to my mind. We were already long past the point when we could have turned back. I just hoped the guys knew what they were doing. I emptied my nervous bladder, retied my scarf to ensure that it was covering every inch of my white face, and resumed my place on the motorcycle.

When we rounded a bend in the road and the police roadblock came into sight, I could hear the blood pounding in my ears. My driver slowed down as if we were going to stop at the barrier. Then, at the very last moment, we both ducked and he drove underneath it, followed almost immediately by Chad, and then Dorgee.

I was straightening up again on the other side when a policeman walked out of the little hut at the edge of the road and looked directly at me. I was certain that the very fact of having my face covered would be enough to arouse his suspicion. But, before he had time to react, we were speeding away into the night. I kept turning round for the next few kilometers, listening for the sound of a siren and expecting to see a pursuing police car. To my surprise and enormous relief, the only vehicles I saw on an otherwise empty dark road were the two motorcycles carrying Chad and Dorgee.

An hour later, there was one more checkpoint to negotiate. My hands were damp with sweat and my heart was racing as we approached it. Surely the message would have got through and the police would be ready and waiting for us. We should turn round and go back. But I knew that wasn't a viable option. And as we couldn't spend the rest of our lives in a no-man's land between two police checkpoints beside the Nujiang River, we had no choice except to carry on.

When we reached the second checkpoint, the village road was being rebuilt and the police station was closed. I felt light-headed with relief as we barreled through and then veered away from the river into the relative safety of the mountains.

An hour after that, we stopped on the mountain trail at a small teahouse. All our bags—containing our tents, sleeping bags, and food—were on the donkeys, which were walking with the guides along the road beside the river and were now probably a whole day behind us. There was no fire burning inside the teahouse. It was very cold and filled with the stench of mushrooms that were being fermented in large containers to sell in the market. I was so tired by that time I would have slept almost anywhere. But there was no room for us in the teahouse.

I was standing on the narrow dirt road trying to focus my mind and think what to do when an SUV pulled up and out of it jumped our cook. She had hired the car and its driver in the first village and brought all our bags and food, leaving the other guides to follow on with the unburdened donkeys. There had been a plan all along; I guess I just hadn't understood it.

Unfortunately, before we had a chance to think about where we were going to pitch our tents for the night, the driver of the SUV— eager to take his money and go home—unloaded all our bags and dumped them at the side of the road. There was nowhere to put up a tent except on the road itself, and we had too many bags to carry them even a short distance to try to find somewhere more suitable.

'You can't just leave us here,' I told the driver. 'Let's put everything back in the car and drive a bit further up the road.' It was clear that he didn't want to bother with us, and although I had already paid him 700 RMB,[2] he demanded more. He did agree in the end though, and drove us to another, apparently abandoned, teahouse. Then, as soon as the bags were unloaded again, he turned his car around and left us in the pitch darkness. It was 01.00, extremely cold, and the only lights we had were a couple of small headlamps.

Our guides didn't have mobile phones, so I went to bed that night not knowing if they would ever find us. We had food and all our gear. But if the donkeys never came, we would have no means of moving it. I was almost beyond the point of exhaustion and there was nothing I could about any of it until the morning.

Our cook went back along the trail to sleep at the first teahouse and by the time I woke up the next morning, she had already returned and was cooking a very welcome breakfast. While we were eating it, the owner of the teahouse we thought was derelict turned up and was delighted to find us camped virtually on his doorstep. I was happy, too, when we discovered that he had a supply of water pumped up by hose from a nearby river. After washing ourselves and drying some clothes, we slept for most of the rest of the day.

Walking in the mountains—as distinct from mountain climbing —isn't really dangerous if you plan it well, take all the necessary precautions, and have an experienced guide. What *is* risky, and emotionally draining, is riding for three hours in the dark on the back of a motorcycle being driven by a 17-year-old. It felt like we had been very lucky, and it was good to be able to rest and recover my equilibrium. In the evening, I sat by the fire in the teahouse and breathed a sigh of relief. What we had done the previous day was stupid, and none of us felt good about it. But it's amazing how a fire can lift your spirits.

We were still sitting in the teahouse when a couple of guys came

2. 700 RMB (Chinese Yuan) is about US$114, or £68.

in and asked where we were going. 'Over the mountain and down to the next village,' I told them.

'You know there's a road now?' one of them said. 'They completed it last year. Do you want us to take you? It's a two-hour ride by motorcycle. We'll do it for 300 RMB[3] each.'

'No thanks,' I told him. 'We prefer to walk with the pilgrims.'

The men smiled. 'There are no pilgrims to walk with,' they said. 'They've all jumped on buses.'

I guess I thought people would travel by vehicle on the stretch of new road that runs along the Nujiang River and then pick up the trail again on the mountain, as we were doing. What the men told us would explain why we hadn't seen a single pilgrim since arriving in the first village the previous day—and why the teahouse owner had greeted us with such enthusiasm. I hadn't realized that the way we were planning to walk would also be on the new road.

What the men were offering to do was take us up the mountain's penultimate pass; then we would walk over it and down the other side. Sometimes, all you can do is roll with the punches. 'Fine,' I said. 'We'll take the bikes.' And we arranged with them to come back for us the next morning.

It wasn't how I wanted my journeys to the sacred mountains to end. It was tempting to regret the building of a road that has brought the pollution of motor vehicles to a previously unspoiled part of the world. But the reality is that the area doesn't exist simply as a pleasant place for tourists and pilgrims to pass through. The people living in those valleys used to have to walk for two days over the mountain just to buy basic commodities like medicines and building materials. Now, there's electricity and transportation, and the local inhabitants have relatively easy access to all the necessities that people living in the modern world take for granted.

I used to wonder why China didn't have more 'protected areas' like the national parks in North America, and why the government doesn't preserve more of its natural environments. Part of the answer is that there are just too many people living in China.

---

3. 300 RMB (Chinese Yuan) is approximately US$50, or £30.

It's easy to preserve land in a sparsely populated area like the American West. In China, the only unpopulated land tends to be inaccessible, or uninhabitable for some other reason.

The path of any *kora* is the path of least resistance—the lowest point of the mountain with the gentlest ascent. And that's also likely to be the best place to build a road. My immediate reaction was to resent the fact that the new road had ruined our trek. In the bigger picture, however, the lives of quite a few people have probably been substantially improved because of it. I was just sorry I wouldn't have any more encounters with pilgrims like the ones I'd enjoyed during the first four days of the journey to Kawa Karpo.

I wondered afterwards what I would have done if we hadn't encountered permit problems. Would I have walked along the road rather than jumping in an SUV? Traveling in a vehicle would have felt like abandoning the final trek, which I know would have been very hard to do. Like a magician showcasing all his tricks, or a market vendor displaying his wares, nature had thrown almost everything she's got at us on our previous journeys—snow, wind, rain, freezing temperatures, tough terrain. And we had coped with it all. It would have been ironic, after all that, to have been defeated simply because I didn't have an official permit. On the other hand, I would have hated walking along a dusty road inhaling the fumes spewed out by passing trucks. So I just don't know the answer.

Because I knew we would be out of internet and mobile phone range for most of the time on all the treks, I had a satellite phone, which meant that I was able to talk to my wife most nights. That night, more than any other, I really needed the boost she gave me.

The journey to Kawa Karpo was turning out to be very different from the way I expected it to be. Despite the obvious benefits the new road had brought for local people, I was saddened by the sense that an incredibly beautiful part of the world had changed forever. But, even in the remote mountains of Tibet, life moves on.

I couldn't understand why none of the pilgrims I talked to during the first few days of the journey had mentioned the road, or the fact that at least half the *kora* now has to be done by car, bus, or motorcycle. I can only assume they didn't see it as a big issue. And maybe it isn't, in the general scheme of things. Maybe the reason why I felt so disheartened that night was simply because the exertions of the last few weeks were starting to take their toll on my mind as well as on my body.

/ 10 \

There were three distinct phases of the journey to Kawa Karpo. In the first, we were faced with the tough physical challenge of walking up to the Duoke La Pass and then down the other side through deep river valleys. The second involved an unanticipated and very unwelcome encounter with the road construction and bureaucracy that is ubiquitous in modern China. And the third began when we returned to the mountain after our clandestine motorcycle ride along the Nujiang River.

The previous night, we set our camp on a slight dip in the ground near the teahouse. When I woke up at 08.00 on the morning of 29 October, the rain that fell throughout the night had pooled and turned the soil under my groundsheet to thick, slimy mud. Although the groundsheet had done its job and kept the inside of the tent dry, it provided no thermal insulation, and the mud was very cold. It was a rough way to wake up. At Mount Kailash, the air and the ground were always dry, even when it was snowing. At Kawa Karpo, the combination of the damp and the very low temperature was a real bone chiller.

We ate breakfast and were in the process of packing up our wet, muddy tents when the guides arrived with the donkeys. Suddenly, it felt as though we were back on track. We were in the mountains and out of reach of the administrative complications that are part of everyday life in China. I was anxious to start walking again. But, first, there was one more, short but almost vertical, motorcycle journey to contend with.

Halfway up the trail to the pass we hit a full-scale snowstorm. I was already caked in wet mud; within a few seconds, I was also incredibly cold. There are many places you don't want to be in heavy snowfall. Exposed on the back of a motorbike on the side of a mountain comes close to the top of the list.

When we reached the high pass, we took refuge in a teahouse, and I sat by the fire waiting for the flames to coax life back into my body and soul. The three motorcycle drivers wore helmets—although there were none for their passengers. But, for some reason, they didn't have gloves. So, before we left the teahouse, I went into the shop and bought a pair for each of them.

The ground on the way up to the high pass was very slippery. That isn't really a problem when you're going uphill—the back wheel of your motorcycle might fishtail, but you're not going to slip and fall as long as you keep the front wheel pretty straight. It's going downhill that's really scary. If you start to slide, it doesn't matter which way you turn the wheel, you're going to go in the direction in which gravity is pulling you. Fortunately, our drivers were far more experienced than the kids who sneaked us through the villages a couple of nights earlier. And once I realized I was in safe hands, it sat back and relaxed into my role as passenger.

The snow was falling thick and fast at the top of the high pass, so we didn't hang around long before beginning our descent on the other side. Once we were below the snowline, we reached my favorite spot of the whole trip—a bend in the river with a fantastic view of the mountains. We continued to follow the river until we came to the small village of Kelbu, where we paid off the drivers and waited for our guides and donkeys to catch up with us again.

Modern cement construction doesn't seem to have reached Kelbu and most of the stucco-fronted houses still have the beautifully carved wooden window frames painted in bright colors that are so typical of old buildings in Tibet.

When the guides arrived, I started knocking on doors looking for somewhere for us to stay, and it wasn't long before we found a family who had room for guests. But although they were happy for Chad and me to stay in their house, and Dorgee, too, after they examined him closely, they refused to allow our guides to set foot inside it. 'People from Yongtsa village are devil worshippers,' they told us later, emphatically and without explanation. So the guides

walked on down the hill and found a teahouse with a less super-
stitious owner.

The flat roofs of most of the houses in the village were covered in
recently harvested corncobs and pumpkins that had been laid out
to dry in the sun. The hospitable family we stayed with very kindly
moved their corn aside for a night so that we could put our sodden,
dirty tents on their roof to dry. Then we explored the village and
did some filming.

When we returned to the house to share the family's evening
meal, they told us about themselves. The household consisted of
a grandmother, four brothers, one wife, and numerous children.
Following an old tradition that used to be common in remote
regions of Tibet, although the children had been fathered by different brothers, they were being raised by all the adults and were
considered to be the progeny of only the oldest brother. The people
are very poor and there is no question of four sons being able to
support their own wives, homes, and families. So they share what
few resources they have, including—as in the case of our hosts—
their women. China's one-child policy never held much sway in
remote villages like Kelbu, and they are off the grid in terms of
judicial or government intervention.

In addition to cooking and cleaning for four 'husbands' and all
the children, the woman of the house works in the fields, while the
men do construction or any other jobs they can find that will provide them with a wage. Now that the route of the *kora* bypasses villages like Kelbu, there are no circumambulating pilgrims looking
for somewhere to stay for the night. As a result, many families have
lost a significant part of what was already a very meager income. So
I was glad to be able to give them some money in exchange for letting us share their food, sleep in their house, and pitch our tents on
their roof. It's a hard existence in that part of the world, and it was
a very positive experience to be on the receiving end of the family's
friendly hospitality—in Kelbu, the village of exhausted wives.

The next part of our journey would be the most challenging yet
and would take us up to the Shula Pass, the last high pass before
we began our descent to the Mekong River. There were more motorcycle taxis in the village and we decided to ride again the next day,

just to the start of the Shula Pass, rather than walk along the road. When we told our guides what we were planning to do, they said, 'That's fine. But we need to leave with the donkeys at 07.00 so that we all end up at the same place at the same time.'

Chad, Dorgee, and I woke up at 06.30 the next morning, packed up our tents and bags, and carried them out on to the road, where we expected our guides to be waiting for us. When the minutes ticked by and they still didn't turn up, Dorgee went down to the teahouse and found them all still fast asleep. We were back on Tibetan time!

I hadn't envisaged doing any part of any of the treks on the back of a 150-cc Ling Feng motorcycle with a radio clamped to its handlebars. It was a surreal experience cruising through stunning river valleys and picturesque villages to the constant, very loud accompaniment of popular music, including the South Korean song 'Gangnam Style.'

We were paying the drivers by the day and they were happy to stop whenever we wanted to film. So it was mid-afternoon by the time we arrived at the small riverside village that marked the final low-altitude point of our journey, at 2900 m (9514 ft). I paid off the motorcycle-taxi drivers and we checked into a small guesthouse before looking around the village of Ganktsa. Basically just a truck stop that has sprung up on the road within the last four or five years, the village consists of a cluster of mostly two-story buildings with restaurants on the first floor and guesthouses above. There were a lot of motorcycles and trucks passing through it, but not a single pilgrim.

We set off quite early the next morning up a steep road to the last village before the Shula Pass. An old woman in the village held a bag of roasted barley above my head and blessed our journey before we set off, on foot at last. After walking 2400 m (7874 ft) up to the pass, which is 5300 m (17,388 ft) above sea level, we were going to have to descend on the other side for at least 1000 vertical-meters (3281 ft) to a more comfortable altitude for sleeping. Dorgee hadn't circumambulated Kawa Karpo before. I had, and I knew just how intense the next part of the trek was going to be.

We walked through trees for most of the morning, up a steep, switchback path. When we reached a plateau at about 4000 m (13,123 ft), the temperature suddenly dropped. By 4500 m (14,764 ft), we had left the trees below us and were walking in the clouds on rocky alpine terrain. And then it started to snow. Even Dorgee found the combination of altitude and walking up almost vertical inclines quite tough. But the local guides took it all in their stride and three of them pushed on, leaving the fourth to stay with us and the camera donkey.

We were about just below the high pass when we stopped to rest at a small, abandoned stone shelter. It was a relief not to have to battle with the elements for a few minutes, and it was a huge boost to find that our guides had already been there and stoked up a fire before they left. I was very grateful for the warmth. It's an unpleasant sensation to be soaked in sweat from head to toe in an air temperature of well below freezing. As I took off my jacket and several layers of clothing to dry them by the fire, clouds of instantly cooled steam rose off my body like smoke.

We sat by the fire in the shelter for about half an hour. It was still snowing when we left, and it continued to snow until we reached the Shula Pass—eight painful, exhausting hours after we left the guesthouse in Ganktsa village. The wind was blowing, as it invariably was on the high passes, and it was too cold to stay up there filming for very long. But it was the tenth and final mountain pass of the last of our four treks around the sacred mountains, so Chad and I took a few minutes to savor the moment. I was shattered: every part of my body ached and I was completely drained of energy. And I was immensely proud of what we had achieved.

The sun was already starting its slow descent behind the mountains as we left the high pass. The snow was even deeper on the other side, and the rocks below it were icy and very slippery. It would have been treacherous ground even if the muscles in my legs hadn't been weakened by fatigue. Dorgee gave me one of his walking poles and Chad used the camera's tripod to support himself. Although I was anxious to find somewhere to camp before it got dark, I knew I mustn't allow my anxiety to color my judgment so that I took risks and made mistakes.

At last, the snow stopped falling. A short distance into the grassland, we rested at another small hut, where, once again, our guides had left a fire burning for us. This time, the cook was there too, to let us know that the others had carried on down the mountain to find somewhere suitable to graze the donkeys and make our camp. I sat by the fire and pulled the water container out of my camelback. For the first time in all my trekking experience, it had frozen into a solid block of ice.

Since setting out on the first trek nearly four months earlier, that day was the longest, toughest day of them all. We ascended an almost vertical 2400 m (7874 ft) and then descended an equally dangerous 1300 m (4265 ft) in 11 hours, walking for the last two of them in total darkness with only the light from our headlamps to illuminate the ground directly in front of our feet. Perhaps the guides hadn't realized we would be so far behind them. Fortunately, when we finally caught up with them, they had already set the camp. Exhausted by effort and stress, I was too tired to eat and went straight to bed.

When you're walking on rough, uneven ground on the side of a mountain in pitch darkness, trying to follow a trail you can't see, you *know* you're doing something stupid. At times like that, it's the adrenalin that keeps you going. When the fear subsides, the adrenalin stops pumping. Then your brain turns its attention to the pain that has been with you every step of the way but that you've been too preoccupied with staying alive to be aware of. That night, despite the pain, a small part of my brain was doing high-fives and telling me, 'If you can get through a day like that, you can do anything.'

There were many occasions when I went to bed feeling wretched and woke up the next morning with my spirits were more or less restored, ready to push on again. But that wasn't what happened on this occasion. When I woke up on day 11, the last day of our complicated, motorcycle-assisted *kora* around Kawa Karpo, I was still too tired to eat. I sat gazing into the fire with the unseeing eyes of total fatigue, drinking coffee, and trying to get warm. I don't think the message my body was sending to my brain could have been any clearer: it had had enough. Unfortunately, I couldn't listen to it yet.

I was so stiff and sore that I could barely bend down to pack up my tent. Before we left the campsite, Dorgee put branches from a pine tree onto the fire to smother the flames and create the pungent smell of incense that's supposed to bring good luck on the last day of a journey. Then we started walking again, descending towards the 'real' world, which had continued to turn on its axis while we were on the mountain.

Snow had been falling all night. When the sun rose high enough in the sky to illuminate the valley, it began to melt, causing the moss-covered rocks and fallen leaves to become wet and slippery under our feet. I walked slowly and very cautiously on the perilous terrain. As the roar of the Mekong River's tumbling waters grew louder, the air temperature began to rise, and the ground became less treacherous. But, even then, my legs were so weak that each step took a huge effort of will. I was beginning to think I might not make it to the end of the trail when I stumbled around a bend and saw a small bridge spanning the river. On the other side of it was the G214 Highway. We had done it!

In some ways, the journey to Kawa Karpo was the most challenging and ultimately satisfying of them all. But it was disappointing, too, because it was the only journey we completed without having seen the sacred mountain. Eleven days earlier, when we stood on the rooftop terrace of the guesthouse in Deqen, it had been shrouded in clouds. Since then, we hadn't caught even a glimpse of it, sometimes due to persistent cloud and sometimes for topographical reasons.

Chad and I were booked on a flight to Shanghai the following afternoon. So we drove to Deqen and stayed that night in the same guesthouse we'd stayed in before we set out on our journey. I felt as though I could sleep for several days, but I forced myself out of bed early the next morning and went out onto the rooftop terrace in the hope of seeing the sun rise one last time. And, suddenly, there it was—the angular snow-capped peak of the sacred mountain of

Kawa Karpo bathed in the golden light of the rising sun. Within seconds, the clouds rolled in again and it was gone.

It was the first time the clouds had broken for several days, the guesthouse owner told us. I felt as though I had been given a gift. After all the subterfuge and motorcycle rides that had marred the trek, it was as if nature was reminding me of what really matters.

The best months to travel to Kawa Karpo are September, October, and November.

The *kora* around Kawa Karpo is the longest and most physically exhausting holy trek in Western China. It can take up to two weeks to complete the 240 km (149 mile) route, which ranges in altitude from 1800 m (5906 ft) in the Mekong River valley to 5300 m (17,388 ft) at the last of six ascents at the Shula Pass.

Having hired a driver and car in Shangri-La (3770 m/12,369 ft), in Yunnan Province, you will have an 8-hour drive to Deqen, where you will start your trek. When you return to Deqen 12–15 days later, you can hire a driver and vehicle for the drive back to Shangri-La.

From Shangri-La, you can fly to Kunming, the capital of Yunnan Province. From Kunming Changshui International Airport, you can fly on to Beijing, Shanghai or Hong Kong.

How to Get to Kawa Karpo

Fly to Shangri-La, Yunnan Province, China.

Drive 8 hours northwest to Deqen.

If possible, spend a night in Deqen and buy supplies for your trek.

Take a taxi south along the Mekong River to Yongtsa village.

Be sure to visit the Kampa Caravan Travel Agency at the top of Yongtsa village. The folks there are great and can help with the hiring of guides and donkeys.

The food at the local Yongtsa market is NOT great—hence the advice above about buying supplies in Deqen.

Potential Costs

The following costs are based on the assumption that you are traveling alone, rather than in a tour group, and were correct in October 2013, when US$1 = 6.15 Yuan.

Flight from Kunming to Shangri-La: 1500 Yuan

Cost of driver and vehicle from Shangri-La to Deqen: 1500 Yuan

Cost of taxi from Deqen to Yongtsa village on Mekong River: 600 Yuan

Cost per donkey: 150 Yuan per day

Cost per donkey handler/guide/cook: 100 Yuan per day

Cost of food: budget for 200 Yuan per person per day

Cost of driver and vehicle from Deqen to Shangri-La: 1500 Yuan

Flight from Shangri-La to Kunming: 1500 Yuan

Note. Costs might fluctuate during high season. Expect to pay more
with a tour group.

How I Completed this Trek
I flew from Shanghai to Kunming to Shangri-La.
I hired a car with driver from Shangri-La to Deqen to Yongtsa.
I hired 1 cook and 2 guides with 6 donkeys.
I hired a private van from Deqen back to Shangri-La.
I flew from Shangri-La to Kunming to Shanghai.

Important note. You should be sure to consult a physician before
attempting any high-altitude trekking. Many pilgrims and travelers
to these regions die each year because of health problems and lack
of preparedness. The risks are REAL.

The End of the Journey

Everybody needs beauty as well as bread,
places to play in and pray in, where nature may heal
and give strength to body and soul.
[JOHN MUIR]

If you look up the word journey in a dictionary, you'll find two apparently distinct definitions: 'an act of traveling from one place to another' and 'a long and often difficult process of personal change and development.' Perhaps they are interdependent more often than we realize. The treks I undertook around some of the most sacred mountains of China certainly proved to be journeys in both senses of the word. For me, though, it was the 'act of traveling' that was the difficult part; the 'personal change and development' occurred without my even noticing.

The idea behind trekking in the sacred mountains was twofold: to challenge myself and to share what I saw and experienced with other people. So, as if walking at high altitude in rain, snow, wind, and mind-numbingly cold temperatures wasn't enough of a test, I took it one step further and the entire adventure was filmed.

When I was in India with my brother in 2012 filming 'The India Ride', we were given a brief lesson in the art of meditation. I rarely sit still unless I'm strapped into the seat of an airplane and I found it incredibly difficult. I realize now that meditation probably has the same effect for many people as walking in the sacred mountains had for me.

Without the distraction of phone calls, emails, meetings to

arrange and attend, flights to book and catch, I reached a point during the treks when all the extraneous debris seemed to clear from my head. It usually occurred after a couple of days: I'd find my rhythm, stop thinking about what lay ahead, and give myself up to the uncomplicated process of walking. Without the trivial concerns that normally occupy so much head space, my mind was free to focus on what really matters to me—my family, aspirations, and dreams.

I controlled every aspect of the planning and organization of the treks until the moment we loaded our bags onto the donkeys and yaks. Then, as we took our first steps along the trail, nature took the reins from my hands. That sense of being at the mercy of something powerful makes you understand why people believe in gods. And in remote regions like the Tibetan Plateau, where else would those gods live except on the unassailable summits of the world's tallest, most majestic mountain ranges?

Even when nature is holding the reins, you still have to make decisions and take responsibility for yourself. Making the wrong decision on the mountains can get you into serious, even fatal, trouble. And overconfidence can kill you, too. From the building of the first pyramid in Egypt more than 4500 years ago, to the construction of the Large Hadron Collider, human beings have shown themselves to be capable of extraordinary achievements in the realms of science, technology, art, and music. But still we remain unable to prevent the earthquakes, volcanic eruptions, tsunamis, and other natural disasters that periodically destroy what we have created. Ultimately, it isn't human beings who are in control and it is prudent to remember that nature will always have the last word, if she chooses to do so.

On the motorcycle circumnavigations of India and China I did with my brother, the greatest risk was from other drivers, of trucks, buses, and cars. Any mistakes they made threatened our lives as well as their own. For the most part though, they were predictable in their unpredictability, and we were able to protect ourselves by riding defensively. On the sacred mountains, it seemed that Mother Nature was more capricious. Sometimes, on the worst days, she appeared to be focusing her undivided attention on harassing us. On the best days, she allowed the sun to shine and showed us some of the most beautiful landscapes in the world.

I didn't find a god on the sacred mountains. I didn't reconsider my attitude towards religion or turn into a born-again, tree-hugging environmentalist in any practical sense. I simply learned how to look into the forest and see each individual tree. And, in the process, I saw the best version of myself. The isolation gave me breathing space and a sense that I am part of something much bigger than my own hopes, dreams, and ambitions. I know I won't always be my 'best version', but knowing what I *can* be gives me something to aspire to, and to focus on so that I can get back on track when I become distracted.

As John Muir said more than 100 years ago, 'Wilderness is not redeemed by man. Man is redeemed by wilderness.' In terms of physical distance, I walked more than 500 km in the mountains in what amounted to less than eight weeks over a period of four months. In terms of 'enlightenment', I traveled light-years.

The peace that exists in remote mountain regions is different from the peace you might find anywhere else. Perhaps it's something to do with the fact that the environment has barely changed for thousands of years and will remain much the same for thousands more to come. It's as if that sense of timelessness creates a bridge between the past and the future. And maybe there's reassurance to be found in the fact that the mountains represent an antithesis to the impermanent world we have created for ourselves.

Walking in the footsteps of the thousands of pilgrims who trod the paths before me gave me a new perspective. The more I travel and the more 'foreigners' I meet, the more aware I become of the similarities between people with apparently very different cultures and ideals. At the root of all our identities are common ancestors whose survival was reliant on their understanding of the natural world. By turning our backs on nature and immersing ourselves exclusively in the modern world, we are separating ourselves increasingly from that shared ancestry. And, in the process, we are widening the gulf between people of different races and creeds. Reconnecting with nature from time to time enables us to re-examine ourselves and gives our spirits space to expand.

> ### Hiking is good for you
>
> According to recent research, including a study reported in the *International Journal of Sports Medicine*, hiking makes you happier and healthier.
>
> It improves people's sense of wellbeing.
>
> It can increase attention span and creative problem-solving skills by as much as 50 percent.
>
> It increases fitness and can reduce the dangers of heart disease, diabetes, and strokes for people at high risk.
>
> It may increase the antioxidative capacity of the blood, thereby improving the body's ability to fight diseases such as cancer.
>
> It can be an effective additional therapy for people suffering from severe depression.

Since returning to Shanghai after the last trek to Kawa Karpo, my life has been as crazily busy as it always was. I still spend too many hours on airplanes and much less time with my family than I'd like to. I haven't changed the way I live: I haven't sold my car, reduced my dependence on technology, or given up any of the trappings of modern urban life. But although my life hasn't changed in any fundamental way, *I* have. In some way I can't explain, I'm more centered than I was a few months ago, as though something inside me has been recalibrated and rebalanced. My thought processes are different, and I spend a great deal more of my time just thinking. In a world where, according to a recent survey in the UK, people use technology devices for an average of 8 hours and 41 minutes a day—and sleep for 20 minutes less—it seems that I might be bucking the trend.

There were days on the treks when I reached the limits of my endurance and when sheer exhaustion made me emotional. But with each breakdown I became stronger. Every time I thought, 'I can't do this; it's too hard,' I heard a voice in my head say, 'You can't give up *now*, after you've come so far. Just stop complaining and keep moving.' And then I realized that the voice was mine.

Now that I know what I'm capable of doing, I have the confidence to decide what I *want* to do and to believe I can take on whatever life throws at me.

I have always been a proponent of the autonomous way of doing business. I admire people who dance to the beat of their own drum, as many of the world's greatest innovators and artists have done. Maybe we would all benefit from stopping every now and then to listen to the sound of our own heartbeat and to remind ourselves that we do have a choice about how we live our lives.

Life has a way of scooping you up and rushing you along to some final destination you don't remember having chosen. For many people, it happens as soon as they finish formal education. Before hurtling blindly along that path, we should heed the words variously attributed to Mark Twain, H. Jackson Brown, and, more probably, to the latter author's mother:

> *Twenty years from now you will be more disappointed by the things you didn't do than by the ones you did do. So throw off the bowlines. Sail away from the safe harbor. Catch the trade winds in your sails. Explore. Dream. Discover.*

Different people find answers to the important questions in different places. I found mine on the slopes and valleys of some of the most sacred mountains in China. For me, being in the mountains feels like going home. It enables me to press the reset button so that I can deal with life, just as I do when I see my family again after having been away too long. The mountains are where I catch the trade winds. But there are many less arduous and less time-consuming ways of exploring, dreaming, and discovering than trekking in remote regions of China. I hope that, by sharing my experiences, other people might be inspired to have adventures of their own.

Acknowledgments

I owe a great deal to all the people who made the *Sacred Mountains of China* expedition possible and to those who have helped and supported us in other ways.

The Sacred Mountains team
Chad Ingraham, Dorgee, Tsering, Kalsang, Jane Smith, TL Lim, Meeyian Yong, David Harris, Alex Stoloff, Jack Woon, Alex Riviere, Jonathan Hogan, Nick Soares, Jeff Berry, and Jonathan Hicks.

Our corporate partners
Mandarin House Language School: Jasmine Bian.
The North Face: Bruno Feltracco, Jacob Uhland, Neville Lin, Hu Hao
Oakley: Nicholas Huang, Alan Peng, Nina Zhang
Zenith Watches: Juliette North, Maud Tiberti, Ivy Tsai, Cyril Bedat.

Books By Ryan Pyle

Chinese Turkestan
Published: Ryan Pyle Productions
ISBN: 978-0992864408
Available: Amazon
Genre: Photography, China

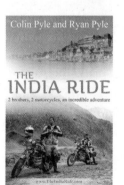

The India Ride
Published: G219 Productions
ISBN: 978-0957576247
Available: Amazon
Genre: Travel, India

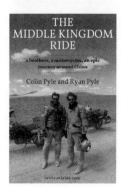

The Middle Kingdom Ride
Published: G219 Productions
ISBN: 978-0957576216
Available: Amazon
Genre: Travel, China

Biography

Born in Toronto, Canada, Ryan Pyle spent his early years close to home. After obtaining a degree in International Politics from the University of Toronto in 2001, Ryan realized a lifelong dream when he traveled to China on an exploratory mission. In 2002, he left Canada and went to live permanently in China. In 2004, he became a regular contributor to the *New York Times* and in 2009, he was listed by *PDN Magazine* as one of the 30 emerging photographers in the world. Since 2010, when Ryan began working full time on television and documentary film production, he has produced and presented several multi-episode television series for major broadcasters in the USA, Canada, UK, Asia, China, and continental Europe.

Recent Awards

2014—Explorer of the Year—Geographical Society of Philadelphia
2013—Awarded Gold Medallion from Governor General of Canada
2012—Guinness World Record—Endurance Motorcycle Riding
2010—PDN Photo Annual—Winner
2009—PDN 30—Emerging Photographer
2009—Magenta Foundation—Flash Forward Emerging Photographer

Television Series

2016—Tough Rides: Brazil (Presenter/Producer)
2015—Extreme Treks: Sacred Mountains of China (Presenter/Producer)
2014—China's Great Gateway: Shaanxi (Presenter/Producer)
2014—Tough Rides: India (Presenter/Producer)
2013—Tough Rides: China (Presenter/Producer)

Affiliations

The Asian Institute–Affiliate Member
The Explorers Club–Member
Guinness World Record Holder–Endurance Motorcycle Riding